HOW TO SURVIVE A SELECT COMMITTEE

HOW TO SURVIVE A SELECT COMMITTEE

SCOTT COLVIN

Biteback Publishing

First published in Great Britain in 2019 by
Biteback Publishing Ltd
Westminster Tower
3 Albert Embankment
London SE1 7SP
Copyright © Scott Colvin 2019

ISBN 978-1-78590-451-6

10 9 8 7 6 5 4 3 2 1

A CIP catalogue record for this book is available from the British Library.

Set in Minion Pro and Steelfish

Printed and bound in Great Britain by
CPI Group (UK) Ltd, Croydon CR0 4YY

To my wife and best friend Hannah

CONTENTS

ACKNOWLEDGEMENTS

It was a great honour for this to be the last book commissioned by Iain Dale before he stepped down from Biteback. I owe him a great debt, as well as Andy McNab, Olivia Beattie and the rest of the Biteback team, especially Ellen Heaney, who helped correct my errors with great patience.

This project could not have happened without the support of Finsbury's chair Roland Rudd, as well as its managing partner James Murgatroyd. I am fortunate to have worked with and to have learned from them both; they are the best in the business.

Huge thanks go to my wonderful family, including my sons Oliver, Kerr and Alexander, for all their support and encouragement when I told them I would be writing a second book.

Thanks to all those former and current committee chairs who gave up their time to be interviewed during the research phase, or provided me with other forms of information, including Rt Hon. Dame Margaret Hodge MP, Rt Hon. Nicky Morgan MP, Dr Sarah Wollaston MP, Rachel Reeves

MP, Crispin Blunt MP, Damian Collins MP and Rt Hon. Sir
Richard Ottaway. Some others wished our conversations to
remain off the record.

Thanks also to the large number of people who provided
illuminating insights and helped along the way, including
Dr Hannah White at the incomparable Institute for Government, Philip Aylett, Sheridan Westlake, John Pienaar,
Duncan McCourt, Andrew Haldenby, Jack Walker and
Stewart Jackson. I also received excellent research support
from Olivia Creavin, Magdalena Gornicka, Elliott Perkins
and Hollie Akehurst at Finsbury.

FOREWORD

Select committees have become a key function of our parliamentary democracy and are one of the key ways of holding to account those in public life.

I was privileged to be the chair of the Foreign Affairs Committee during the years of the coalition government, and it remains the most rewarding position I held in my thirty-two years in Parliament.

During my time leading the committee's work, it was evident that it was often the most effective means for the public to get answers to great issues of the day. The media's questions are frequently batted back; public inquiries can be kicked into the long grass; but select committees command respect because they represent the collective voice of millions of citizens around the country and can act with great speed.

However, it is also true that the select committee system could be improved. In the race to be first, and to sometimes play to the cameras while doing so, committees can create distrust in their intentions, encouraging witnesses to prevaricate and to be guarded to the point of rendering their appearance wholly unsatisfactory.

If we are going to have a select committee process which continues to explore relevant issues of the day in a detailed and forensic way, we need to reflect on the level of resourcing Parliament provides, and ensure that current and future chairs have all the tools required. We also need to ensure that witnesses have confidence that they will be given a fair hearing.

This book, remarkably the first to focus solely on select committees, takes an extensive look at the history of the committee system, why they continue to strike fear into the hearts of senior executives and what the future holds. Perhaps most importantly, the book will provide a practical guide to how to survive a select committee with your reputation intact and potentially even enhanced.

I have known Scott Colvin for many years and I have great respect for his ability to understand how parliamentarians think, and what motivates and drives them. He has advised many senior people on how best to deal with the challenges posed by select committees. His analysis in this book is presented in an accessible way with many thoughtful ideas about how the current system can be improved, and thus safeguard the ability of Parliament to ask the challenging questions so often demanded by constituents and the wider public.

Rt Hon. Sir Richard Ottaway, chair, Foreign Affairs Committee
2010–15

INTRODUCTION

I have many reasons to be grateful for the existence of parliamentary select committees. The sheer terror they create in high-profile individuals and organisations means that I have frequently been hired to help support them through a process which can be incredibly arduous. Across the various communications advice I dispense in my day job, it is assistance with select committees for which senior people are most grateful.

Preparing people for committee hearings is also, however difficult for the witness, the most fun and intellectually stimulating part of my role. That is because select committees are like no other experience. They are akin to a mini-crisis with very clear time limits and huge potential threats to the person or organisation in the firing line.

In the near-decade since membership of select committees was based on an election rather than party selection, they have significantly increased in profile. Matching the rise of populism in our wider society, the committee chairs have begun to reshape expectations of the role and are using it to drive a far more combative approach. More than seven years after the event, many people still remember the car-crash appearances of the US firms accused of tax dodging by former Public Accounts Committee chair Margaret Hodge. The reputation of those companies has never quite recovered. Although we may still value the jobs they bring or the innovations they deliver, our perceptions of Google, Amazon and Starbucks changed for ever. No media interview, even led by a formidable journalist such as Jeremy Paxman or John Humphrys, could have achieved that level of success.

After decades of being relatively unexciting, in recent years select committees have become a terrifying experience for powerful people in our public life. The committees' findings and recommendations may often be ignored, they may even be dismissed – but they are always feared. However, it is not just ministers and senior government officials who must endure the scrutiny of the committees. Increasingly, the private sector is being held to account in an even more aggressive and challenging way.

In my experience, senior executives are adept at handling even tricky annual general meetings (AGMs) with shareholders and they are able, albeit with some support, to appear before the cameras and deliver a good broadcast interview. Both of these challenging corporate moments can be controlled, to a certain extent. The AGM is hosted by the company, so it can control the venue, the attendees, the agenda and who gets to speak, for example. While media interviews are clearly less easy to control, you know that survival can often be a matter of enduring the few minutes that the journalist has to ask you questions. You are also not obliged to appear on the *Today* programme or *Newsnight*; it is a choice.

But select committees are different. They push you out of your comfort zone. As you take your seat, you are all too aware that there is a camera trained directly on your face, which can expose your nervousness, emphasising any gulps, poor eye contact or fidgety hands. You are then confronted by up to fifteen parliamentarians across party divides who are generally not going to be on your side and are, sometimes, actively hostile. Despite any pre-briefing from the committee's officials, you have little certainty about the questions you are going to be asked.

If your company has recently suffered a catastrophic IT failure, you may safely assume that the inquiry session will ask questions about the disruption to your customers. However, you may not have predicted that this issue will then lead to an intense round of questioning about where you live, how much you are paid, whether you will accept your bonus and why there are not any women on your board. Even if you survive the hearing, the committee may still get you weeks or months later with a final report which can criticise you freely.

As we continue through these extraordinary times of minority government and political disquiet driven by Brexit, we should ask ourselves whether we are proud of how our select committees currently work, or whether the process has gone too far and is in danger of damaging the standing of Parliament. I strongly believe that select committees matter a great deal and that the broad structure, first developed in 1979, remains a vital tool of democracy. They hold to account the great and powerful, and they ask questions to which many of us would like answers, such as 'How did this go so wrong?' and 'How can we make it better?' If you look across the world and see how other similar countries manage the committee process, we remain a leader and excel in this type of scrutiny.

However, this does not mean that the committees are beyond reproach. In recent years, despite an increase in joint committee inquiries, the competition between them has become more intense and has arguably led to an increase in posturing and dramatic behaviour. This brings into question whether they are always focused on serving the public good.

From the perspective of business leaders, committees feel as though they are designed to jump on any topic of the day to secure a headline, rather than aiming to get a better understanding of how business works and how it can be improved for the benefit of the public. Many of those I interviewed from the private sector said that the committee process did not feel constructive or even well informed. They complain that committees often completely miss the key issues at hand, favouring instead moments of drama. The committees have been successful in creating fear – but should this be the aim of any select committee? You might argue that select committees should indeed be tough, because they are forensic, policy-focused sessions holding powerful people to account – but that's rather different from inspiring panic by throwing out curveball questions.

The committees need to be clear what their ultimate purpose is, and I feel that is currently lacking. They can be successful vehicles for personal ambition and are often very good at grabbing headlines, but they are not always successful in getting to the real heart of the matter. Unlike the role of the official opposition, select committees are not there to simply oppose, so there is no requirement to always choose populism as an approach. They are there to shadow the work of the relevant department(s) and this requires a commitment to quality – more so than we currently see.

Let us get our committees better trained, armed with better questions and encouraged to explore more thoughtful areas of discussion. They need to stop choosing the cheap and lazy questions, such as beating people up on the issue of their pay or bonuses, unless it has direct relevance to the public purse. Rather than trying so hard to get a soundbite on BBC News, let us instead get the findings into the serious media and academic journals.

The select committees should be an even greater source of pride. We should be equivalent to the Premier League in this regard, admired and replicated worldwide. However, we have reached a point where it has become necessary to review our select committee system to ensure it is delivering the best it can for our democracy. Although it has made significant progress since 2010, the jury is out as to whether this momentum can be maintained by a system which is already at full stretch.

From the perspective of MPs on the committees, especially chairs, it is apparent that the pressures of staying elected and progressing one's political career create a huge incentive to structure the committee sessions in this combative way. The committees are generally under-resourced and often lack the expertise required to get the best from the process. This has a direct impact on our democracy. Let us give the committees all the tools they need to make this happen and then ensure they are also held to account so we are getting value for money. It could be one of the most beneficial investments that we make in our politics.

One major element that needs urgent resolution is to better define the powers the committees have to force witnesses to appear before them. Vote Leave guru Dominic Cummings's refusal to appear to give evidence to the Digital, Culture, Media and Sport Committee panel simply exposed the weakness of the current system. Ultimately, if a UK citizen simply refuses to appear, then there is not much that the chairs can do other than huff and puff. This does not seem a satisfactory way forward. But, rather than limp on with an opaque system, we need to shine a light on it and give the committees what they actually need to get the right information. However, they must accept that added powers come with a responsibility to use them appropriately.

For all these reasons, it feels timely to explore what the committees are, what they do, how they could be improved and how to survive them. The time you give to rigorous preparation is one of the best investments you will make. There may well be complete naturals who can walk straight into the committee room with no training and deliver a perfect performance, but in all honesty, I have not met that person over the past twenty years. The poorest performers are often those who either have scant regard for the validity of the select committee process or just think they know everything.

With this book, I hope to ensure you get the best out of the gruelling process. It might just save your reputation.

PART 1

SELECT COMMITTEES
– THE BASICS

'If you ever live in a country run by a committee, be on the committee.'
WILLIAM SUMNER
, AMERICAN POLITICAL SCIENTIST

WHAT IS A SELECT COMMITTEE AND WHY DO THEY MATTER?

A crucial part of the work of the House of Commons and the House of Lords takes place in committees, made up of MPs or Lords. A select committee is a cross-party group of MPs or Lords (and very occasionally both) which is given a specific remit by Parliament to conduct inquiries and produce reports on a range of matters, from the conduct of government to topical issues. This book will primarily focus on those committees operating within the House of Commons, and especially those which are responsible for monitoring government departments.

There is no single way of categorising select committees. However, according to the classification made by the respected think tank the Institute for Government:

- Almost half (nineteen) of Commons committees are departmental, examining the expenditure, administration and policy of a specific department and its associated public bodies.

5

- Cross-cutting committees (six) look across Whitehall to examine government performance on a single issue.
- Legislative committees (five) undertake tasks in relation to the legislative process.
- Domestic committees (nine) facilitate some aspect of parliamentary process, or administration of the House of Commons.

The departmental committees are:

- Business, Energy and Industrial Strategy
- Defence
- Digital, Culture, Media and Sport
- Education
- Environment, Food and Rural Affairs
- Exiting the European Union
- Foreign Affairs
- Health and Social Care
- Home Affairs
- Housing, Communities and Local Government
- International Development
- International Trade
- Justice
- Northern Ireland Affairs
- Scottish Affairs
- Transport
- Treasury
- Welsh Affairs
- Work and Pensions

Additionally, there are a number of committees which have a broader remit. Depending on the issue under consideration, they can look at any or all government departments, including:

- Environmental Audit
- European Scrutiny
- Public Accounts
- Regulatory Reform
- Science and Technology
- Women and Equalities

All of the select committees aim to hold decision-makers accountable by gathering evidence from ministers, officials, the public and organisations outside of Parliament, and publishing a report of their findings, to which the government must respond. These committees consider policy issues, scrutinise the work and expenditure of the government, and examine proposals for primary and secondary legislation. They also, increasingly, focus on the behaviour of companies and private individuals on issues of purported national relevance.

The number of select committees has remained relatively stable in recent years, with the exception of new additions to the roster, such as the Women and Equalities Committee.

Select committees provide one of the primary opportunities for the public to hear directly from the people who shape our daily lives. This could include ministers who take decisions on the running of the NHS; train operators whose services we rely upon to get to work; supermarket bosses who provide our food on our high streets; outsourcing companies which run our prisons; or energy companies which power our homes. Without the committees, these people would find it easier to hide away and it would be more difficult to hold them to account.

In recent years scrutiny has increased significantly and committee chairs such as Margaret Hodge, Keith Vaz and Andrew Tyrie have become household names. Coverage of individual committees more than tripled between 2008 and 2012, and a study led by Professor Meg Russell and Meghan Benton at UCL estimates that between 30 and 40 per cent of select committee recommendations end up as government policy,[1] which represents a much clearer way for a backbench MP to influence the direction of policy than other traditional methods, such as tabling a private member's bill that has only the slimmest chance of becoming law.

The growing attraction of select committees is that they feel as though they are on our side, at a time when politicians generally are seen to be out of touch and out for themselves. Freed from having to supinely suck up to their party leader in order to make ministerial or shadow ministerial office, select committee chairs and members can speak honestly and challenge policy. In many instances, they are led by people who actually have experience in the area they cover. For example, Sarah Wollaston, chair of the Health and Social Care Committee, worked in the NHS for twenty-four years; Tom Tugendhat, chair of the Foreign Affairs Committee, served in the army in both Iraq and Afghanistan;

and Neil Parish, chair of the Environment, Food and Rural Affairs Committee, used to be a farmer.

Some select committees also hold hearings regarding appointments to senior public offices, in which we would otherwise have no say. Although the committees do not yet have the formal power to veto people to whom they object, they at least act as our watchdog.

HISTORY

THE EARLY DAYS

Although we tend to think of parliamentary committees in a modern context, they have existed for centuries. Parliament has long delegated tasks to small groups of members, increasing its capacity and enabling certain members to scrutinise specific issues of public policy, or to examine scandals or disasters.

In this aspect of my research I leaned heavily upon committee historian and current Environment, Food and Rural Affairs Committee clerk Philip Aylett. In his thesis, 'Thirty Years of Reform: House of Commons Select Committees, 1960–1990',[2] he notes that during the sixteenth century, committees became increasingly relied upon to revise bills, as well as a range of other tasks, such as considering constitutional and religious questions of the day.

However, even back then, the independence of the committees was often called into question. As Aylett suggests, 'sixteenth and seventeenth century committees, as small closed bodies working away from the open forum of the floor of the House, were sometimes criticised as being too open to manipulation from outside, and particularly from Ministers seeking to get their way by exerting pressure or promising favours'. This belief that parliamentary committees were often blunted by inappropriate government influence has only recently gone away; from 2010, chairs have been elected by all members of the House of Commons, which has led to more maverick and independently minded MPs taking control. Previously, chairs were selected by political party managers, with little transparency.

Although much of the published history of select committees fails to look back beyond the creation of departmental committees in 1979, the committee system has a colourful and rich past. In particular, it had something akin to a golden age during the nineteenth century, which saw important developments in the House's approach to committee inquiry. As Aylett describes:

There were many select committees on policy and administration matters in the newly-reformed House of the 1830s and 1840s … The 1847–48 Report from the Select Committee on Public Business noted that there were no fewer than 44 select committees on such business in the 1847–48 Session, with an average of 15 members to each committee; they covered subjects ranging from Commercial Distress to Divorce Bills and Highways to Navy, Army and Ordnance Expenditure. Some sat for over 35 days in the Session. Along with this went 28 election committees (to decide on disputed elections), and over 140 groups and committees on private and railway Bills.[3]

Perhaps the longest-lasting legacy given to us by this era was the creation of the Committee of Public Accounts (now often referred to as the 'PAC') in 1861, which has in recent times been seen as the most powerful of all the select committees, thanks to the work of the redoubtable Margaret Hodge, Edward Leigh and David Davis. The PAC's role has always been to 'examine the accounts showing the appropriation of the sums granted to Parliament to meet the public expenditure',[4] an issue which has remained politically important since its inception, regardless of the ebbs and flows of other public policy. This has enabled it to remain a key fixture of the work of Parliament. Aylett describes the foundation of the PAC as 'a very important step towards the institutionally permanent "policy and administration" investigatory committees that developed in the twentieth century'.

However, after this flourishing of the committee system came a gradual but prolonged decline, as select committees fell out of favour. The more divisive the politics became, the greater the scepticism grew towards high-profile and contentious inquiries.

To support the idea that our current system of select committees has been a result of an evolutionary, rather than revolutionary, process, Aylett explains that even in the early twentieth century politicians put forward proposals for the development of a system of committees which would subject the overall policy and administration of government departments to continuous and systematic scrutiny: 'Even at the lowest point of recorded select committee activity, however, between about 1945 and the early 1960s, there appears to have been a clear sense among both frontbench and backbench Members that select committees, once appointed, had the right to decide how to interpret their own remits.' This view was supported by a very influential political figure and surprising hero of the modern select committee system: Harold Wilson.

You may be surprised to learn that the two-time Labour Prime Minister was such a cheerleader of parliamentary scrutiny, but he was a very active and forensic chair of the PAC. He described its work in 1961 in these terms: 'Perhaps it is not going too far to say that the Public Accounts Committee is the only blood sport which is sanctioned by Parliament and which is enjoined upon a select number of its hon. Members as a parliamentary duty.'[5] Judging by the feedback I get from corporate witnesses today, they would conclude that little has changed.

Even more notably, Wilson devoted part of a keynote speech in July 1964, just before that year's general election campaign started, to describing the work of select committees:

In the past year or two, we have seen how effective certain Select Committees – Estimates, Public Accounts, Nationalised Industries – have been at getting to the heart of some national problem by summoning witnesses, taking evidence and reaching agreed conclusions, cutting right across Party controversies. I believe this could be taken further.[6]

Although Wilson remained a passionate advocate of empowered select committees, it would be another fifteen years before they began to take the shape we know today.

THE 1979 REFORMS

The current select committee structure was implemented in 1979 when the then Conservative Leader of the House, Norman St John-Stevas – a much maligned Tory 'wet' who subsequently fell out with his leader Margaret Thatcher – oversaw the creation of the departmental committee system, shadowing different areas of the government, and focused on spending, policies and administration. This was following a report made by the House of Commons Procedure Committee a few years before. It is worth noting that the report was seen by the committee's own members as evolutionary rather than revolutionary. The fact that the reforms of 1979 came to be regarded by some commentators as an epoch in committee history was a view arguably based more on spin than on substance.

Despite being a passionate believer in select committee reform, Stevas was fully aware that the conservative forces in Parliament could scupper the implementation of the reforms. There was significant cynicism in the few years prior to the changes being introduced, perhaps most forcefully expressed by the Labour Leader of the House (and future party leader), Michael Foot, who was 'suspicious of select committees, partly because they work on a non-partisan basis'.[7]

However, it was not just senior Labour figures who wanted to quash the reforms being proposed by the Procedure Committee. Michael Foot also told the then Prime Minister, James Callaghan, in December 1976 that 'the official Opposition, through the usual channels, expressed very limited enthusiasm for the Committee and would happily have seen it forgotten'. This lack of enthusiasm was apparently shared by Margaret Thatcher, who initially thought departmental committees would increase, not put pressure on, government spending. Aylett believes that another reason why there was resistance to change was because of the poor example set by the US Senate investigative committee, which was notoriously chaired by Joseph McCarthy to root out communist influence in American institutions. The committee clerks were apparently determined to avoid 'shades of Cohn and Schine', a reference to McCarthy's aggressive advisors during those sessions. It certainly seemed a very un-British approach to appoint powerful chairs to pursue such specific and targeted agendas unchecked.

In October 1977, the Procedure Committee met and agreed, in outline, the proposals it would put to the House about the future structure of select committees. They included:

1. The Expenditure Committee and its sub-committees, together with most other existing investigative select committees, should be replaced by a series of twelve new select committees 'each charged with the examination of all

aspects of expenditure, administration and policy in a field of administration within the responsibilities of a single government department or two or more related departments'.

2. Nominations for the membership of the new committees should be entrusted to the all-party Committee of Selection, rather than the whips.

3. All departmental estimates should be referred to departmental select committees.

4. Select committee chairs should be paid an additional salary.

5. They should be able to appoint specialist advisors and seek advice from the Exchequer and Audit Department (the forerunner of the National Audit Office).

6. Select committees should be given strengthened powers and clearer enforcement procedures to help them in the vital task of securing access to information held by the government. Select committees' exercise of the existing powers in this area were, the report said, hampered 'by their inability to order the attendance of Ministers or to order the production of papers by at least the great majority of government departments' and by the absence of 'any effective means' of enforcement.[8]

The Procedure Committee report was finally debated on the floor of the Commons in February 1979, and as then shadow Leader of the House (the election followed in May), Stevas said that the 'function of controlling and checking the Executive is not being performed by Parliament as it should be. We have, in effect, a professional Government and we still have an amateur legislature.' He urged the government to put down motions for the establishment of the departmental committees and let the House decide.

Michael Foot was not persuaded, once again arguing against a more powerful committee system:

If we set up the 12 Committees to examine the matters proposed in the report on a regular basis we shall have not merely a further draining away of attention from the Chamber ... but the strength of Parliament being increasingly transferred to such Committees, thereby injuring the position of individual Members.

On 25 June 1979, Stevas opened the House's debate on the Standing Orders establishing the new committees. He said:

Today is, I believe, a crucial day in the life of the House of Commons. After years of discussion and debate, we are embarking upon a series of changes that could constitute the most important parliamentary reforms of the century ... One truth abides and that is that parliamentary government has been one of the great contributions of the British nation to the world's civilisation, and we would do well to remember that.

However, as previously suggested, this rhetoric was somewhat overplayed, and the reforms were never intended to be fundamental. Aylett suggests that the new departmental committees were 'almost a sheep in wolf's clothing', matching the general lack of enthusiasm for something radical and representing incremental change disguised as revolutionary reform.[9]

The 1979 reforms did not deliver on many of the key recommendations of the Procedure Committee, including stronger and clearer powers for select committees, guaranteed Chamber debates and the use of evidence-taking in legislative committees. They were either not implemented or not implemented fully at any time during the following decade. As Aylett concludes:

> These recommendations and others could have made a big difference to the relationship between the government and Parliament, but, in the event, the new committees basically preserved the constitutional status quo. It is indeed interesting and ironic that some of the positive press coverage of the report focussed on precisely these challenging but unimplemented Procedure Committee recommendations. Some of the big headlines and laudatory editorials of August 1978 were therefore giving a warm welcome to reforms that did not actually happen for many years.

What these reforms did, though, was elevate the perception of select committees as a powerful parliamentary tool. This heightened public profile meant that committee activity was even occasionally newsworthy, and published information from select committees became ever more detailed – this has doubtless played its role in exaggerating the significance of 1979.

THE 2009 REFORMS

The more significant changes arguably came in 2009 as a result of the reforms promoted by the former Labour MP for Cannock Chase Tony Wright. The Reform of the House of Commons Committee (known informally as the Wright Committee) was set up in 2009 as part of a wider attempt to improve the antiquated procedures and increase the relevance of Parliament. The final report, in a document entitled 'Rebuilding the House', was published in November 2009.[10]

The long period of majority Labour government before 2010 (which secured majorities of 179, 167 and 65 consecutively) had been marked by a growing concern that the relationship between Parliament and the Executive was unbalanced. Increasingly, the government was making important policy announcements outside, rather than inside Parliament. The Commons therefore felt like a means of merely rubber-stamping decisions that had already been agreed.

The general theme of the Wright Reforms was that the House should have much more scope to choose and schedule its own activities. For example, it concluded that backbench business should be scheduled by the House, rather than by ministers, and one backbench motion per month should be routinely scheduled for debate, including an e-petitions system allowing the public to trigger debates on topics of specific interest. This latter initiative has remained popular with the public, with a range of petitions forcing parliamentary debate, especially on issues related to Brexit.

However, the report also included some eye-catching measures on the format of select committees. These included:

- A reduction in the number of committees and in the size of a standard departmental committee, possibly to eleven members.
- Chairs of departmental and similar select committees should be directly elected by secret ballot of the House using the alternative vote system.
- Members of departmental and similar committees should be elected from within party groups by secret ballot.

In May 2010, the incoming coalition government agreed to bring forward the Wright Committee's recommendations in full, having already been voted through by MPs across the House on 4 March in the dying days of the previous Labour government.

HOW DO THEY FUNCTION?

COMMONS VS LORDS

The House of Lords select committee system slightly differs from their colleagues' in the so-called lower house. They tend to cover more general areas, without the direct departmental shadowing that we see in the Commons. However, the Commons and Lords committee systems are ultimately designed to complement each other.

The six investigative committees in the Lords, which are supported by a range of sub-committees, are:

- Communications (which covers the media and creative industries).
- Constitution (which examines public bills for their constitutional impact).
- Economic Affairs (which considers economic issues).
- European Union (which examines EU documents and other related matters).

- International Relations (which looks at the UK's relationships across the world).
- Science and Technology (which examines issues related to science, engineering, technology and research).

According to the Institute for Government, 'the large membership of the Lords means demand for committee roles is high. It is uncommon for peers to sit on more than one committee – of 780 active Lords, 199 (25 per cent) sit on a committee, and of those just forty-one (5 per cent) sit on more than one.'[11]

I interviewed a number of senior private sector witnesses who have appeared before the committees of both houses, and all reported that the experiences were very different. One witness told me: 'The Lords, while still tough, was a more forensic experience and there was a sense that they genuinely cared about getting to the facts. The Commons committee, on the other hand, was childish, focused on showboating and, I felt, lacking a real understanding of the issues.'

A sweeping generalisation, of course, but it is often felt that peers are not as concerned about making a name for themselves. They are less prone to courting attention (especially as they are not defending constituencies), and instead tend to be more focused on the policy detail.

There is also an obvious difference between those who occupy the two Houses of Parliament. Although there has been an increase in younger peers in recent years (the current Leader of the Lords, Baroness Evans, is only in her early forties), it is generally the case that they are at a more advanced stage of their career, often having served as an MP. For example, the average age of the Commons following the 2017 general election was fifty years old; in the Lords it was sixty-nine years old.

JOINT COMMITTEES

Joint committees operate in the same way as Commons and Lords select committees, but they are made up of members from both houses who meet and work as one committee. They appoint a single chair, who can be an MP or a peer.

There are essentially two types of joint committee. Permanent joint committees conduct an ongoing examination of a particular area. There are currently three fulfilling this role, looking into human rights, national security strategy and statutory instruments. Temporary joint committees meet on specific topics, like those set up to consider draft bills and other issues, and they stop meeting once they have completed their report. Recent examples include the joint committees on the draft Modern Slavery Bill, privacy and injunctions, and prisoner voting.[12]

BECOMING A CHAIR

Although the emergence of the departmental committees in 1979 had improved the scrutiny of government departments, becoming a committee chair (or even a humble member) was still seen as a consolation prize in the absence of frontbench preferment. Government managers, known as whips, handed out these roles as prizes to those they wanted to reward for loyalty or to dampen their potential rebellion. There is a financial carrot too, given that the chair of a select committee receives extra money for doing the job (currently £15,598 per year on top of an MP's basic salary of £79,468).

The huge downside to the previous whip-controlled system was that select committees could be easily bullied or overridden. Committee chairs may be pulled to one side and gently warned that too much scrutiny would not be good for their longevity in the role. This lack of power meant that attendance rates were poor, and committees were rarely in the headlines as often as they are today. While individual committee inquiries had come to prominence, the select committee process as a whole was generally low-key.

One of the most crucial changes implemented as a result of the Wright Report was that committee chairs were to be voted in by a majority of all MPs, meaning that more independently minded candidates were most likely to succeed. As such, the election of chairs by the whole House could be seen as the most significant change to select committees in living memory.

The result has been a radically improved system of scrutiny, as chairs can no longer be threatened with deselection if they are seen as being too challenging. They therefore have the freedom to criticise government departments, national institutions such as the BBC and even powerful business interests.

Since the Wright Reforms, maverick chairs such as Margaret Hodge, Keith Vaz and Damian Collins have adopted a much more populist approach. This has resulted in more newsworthy moments than at any similar period in the history of parliamentary committees. Select committees are therefore increasingly used by MPs as a means to generate media attention around a particular issue, as well as for political posturing and profile-raising. One chair even went so far as to say this is no longer a choice: 'You need to secure coverage for your committee, otherwise you will not survive as chair. It is core to the job.'

As chairs become ever more high-profile, and being a junior minister is increasingly seen as a thankless role by ambitious MPs, select committees have become a genuine career option for parliamentarians.

The election of committee chairs has seen an even higher competition for places. Admittedly, a number of chair positions were not contested after the 2017 general election, but this is probably because a number of chairs had only recently been elected to that role, given the foreshortened 2015–17 parliament. After the last election, seventeen out of twenty-eight elected chairs were not contested. But, where there was freedom to compete, the competition was fierce. In particular, two of the so-called prosperity committees – Treasury and Business, Energy and Industrial Strategy – saw entertaining contests. Former Education Secretary Nicky Morgan went head-to-head with high-profile backbench favourite Jacob Rees-Mogg to become chair of the Treasury Committee, with Morgan emerging victorious; on the Business, Energy and Industrial Strategy Committee, Rachel Reeves saw off the threat of former Labour minister Liam Byrne (whose campaign was probably not helped by the fact he had left a 'joke' note to his Liberal Democrat successor at the Treasury, revealing: 'I'm afraid there is no money. Good luck!').

More than ever (partly because the two main political parties have pulled away from the centre in recent years) we now
see committee chairs who would normally be in very senior
government or shadow Cabinet positions. Four of the current
chairs are former Secretaries of State, eight are former ministers and eight served in the shadow Cabinet.[13] One of the
benefits, according to the Institute for Government, has been
that 'the election of these former ministers has injected greater
understanding of government into the Commons select committee system. It has also helped increase media attention to
committees' work, which in turn has enhanced their influence.'
In short, chairing a committee can provide an independent
platform within Parliament, which can in turn keep a chair's
reputation 'warm' until the political deep freeze thaws.

This independence does, however, have consequences for
the internal workings of committees. Some chairs are now
more likely to follow their own agenda, calling for inquiries
without necessarily getting the approval of committee members. In August 2017, months before the committee was technically able to trigger inquiries, Work and Pensions chair
Frank Field started investigating the Universities Superan-
nuation Scheme's trustee board in relation to its deficit.[14]

Similarly, as soon as Business, Energy and Industrial
Strategy Committee chair Rachel Reeves was elected to the
role in July 2017, she chose to outline the committee's agenda
before a single other member had been elected:

As a Committee, there are a number of issues I believe we
will want to consider for future inquiries. Ensuring that we

develop sustainable growth and climate change policies that help create new and well paid jobs should be a priority for the Committee. Shining a light on diversity at the top levels of our businesses and tackling the gender, disability and BAME pay gaps should be on the Committee's agenda. Scrutinising the Government's approach to the challenges of the 'gig economy' and the growth of self-employment and how to deliver fairness and flexibility in the British labour market should also be an area of interest for the Committee.[15]

The selection system still has its critics. When the Conservative MP Johnny Mercer sought (unsuccessfully) to become the chair of the Defence Committee in summer 2017, he wrote a hard-hitting opinion piece in *The Times*. He complained:

When I started this campaign, I thought that this would come down to a straight shoot out over which candidate MPs preferred. It is disappointing that an active campaign is being conducted by local Labour Party colleagues and ex-colleagues here in Parliament, to deny me a 'platform', with a view to winning my seat for themselves.[16]

It could therefore be argued that successful chairs are not just voted in because they are popular across party divides, but also because there are other Machiavellian motivations at play.

Once elected, the rules stipulate that (unless the House of Commons otherwise decides) a select committee chair can only serve in that role for two parliamentary terms, or a continuous period of eight years, whichever is longest.

PARTY SPLIT

The distribution of chairs depends on the number of committees which are agreed by the House. In the 2015–17 parliament there were a total of twenty-five committees whose chairs were elected.[17] Of the current elected chairs, there are twelve Conservative, twelve Labour, two Scottish National Party, one Liberal Democrat and one independent. (Although there is technically no position for an independent MP, Sarah Wollaston defected to the Independent Group from the Conservative Party during her tenure as Health Committee chair, and at the time of writing has remained in position.)

A committee that has a chair with an aggressive manner, especially if they are also from an opposition political party, can have significant consequences for the department(s) they shadow. As a senior civil servant told me off the record, 'The tougher the chair shadowing a department, the harder life will often become for us and our ministers, so we definitely have our fingers crossed during the ballot.'

The broad principle is that the balance of committee chairs should reflect the party balance in the House of Commons, although there is some flexibility to accommodate difficult electoral outcomes. Once the number of seats won by each party in a general election is revealed, the Speaker's office applies a formula to work out how many chairs should be allocated to each party.

According to the Institute for Government's analysis:

The party whips are informed of the number of chairs to

which they are entitled and negotiate between themselves about which chair should be allocated to which party. Under Standing Orders the Public Accounts Committee has to be chaired by an opposition member. Treasury, Defence and Foreign Affairs are often taken by the government but there is no rule that this has to be the case. Parties will try to get the committees responsible for the policy areas in which their political priorities lie ... The result of the whips' negotiation must then be agreed by the House.[18]

Although you would assume that the party loyalties of the elected chair would be one of the key factors in how a committee conducts itself, it actually tends to be less important than the ability of the chair to inspire loyalty amongst his or her members. For example, some of the most positive comments I have heard about Margaret Hodge's time leading the Public Accounts Committee have been from right-wing Conservative MPs who served alongside her.

DECIDING MEMBERSHIP

Not all MPs can sit on select committees, though it is difficult to build up a complete picture of who is ineligible. The Institute for Government estimates that of the 500 MPs eligible to sit on select committees, around two-thirds – 323 – currently do. It suggests, 'Of these 323, the majority will sit on only one committee.'[19] MPs who are also ministers or shadow ministers are not allowed to sit on departmental select committees, although there is an exemption for the relevant ministers who sit on the Public Accounts Committee and Environmental Audit Committee. However, those ministers do not attend the sessions, despite their right to do so.

All these rules are based upon conventions which may seem indecipherable to those outside of Parliament. Some examples are provided here by the Institute for Government:

> When 56 MPs from the SNP were elected to Westminster in 2015, the distribution formula entitled them to a seat on each Commons committee. But to fulfil this, some of the party's spokespeople doubled up as committee members. Currently some of the leaders of other small parties in Westminster also sit on committees. The role of Parliamentary Private Secretaries has always been contentious – broadly it is applied so that they may not be a member of a committee scrutinising ministers with whom they are directly associated … on some committees the Official Opposition or the Government will 'lend' a seat to a minor party (for example Labour have lent a seat on the Environmental Audit Committee to the Green MP Caroline Lucas and the Conservatives have ceded places on the Northern Ireland Affairs Committee to the DUP).

The process of electing wider committee members begins once the results of the elections for chair have been announced, simply to ensure that unsuccessful candidates can stand. After the rules changed in 2010, the House announced that individual political parties should arrange for their members of select committees to be elected 'in a secret ballot by whichever transparent and democratic method they choose.'[20] All parties use a slightly different method, according to their own agreed process; in 2010, both Labour and Conservative used a two-stage process, which took around a month to conclude. Following elections within parties, the successful candidates are formally proposed to the House by the Committee of Selection, which is usually a straightforward process.

As with the chairs, the party balance of committee membership tries to reflect the seat composition in the House of Commons. So, in an era of tight elections resulting in a government without a working majority, a typical committee might have five Conservatives, five Labour members and one minority party representative. In the event that a minority party cries foul at the prospect of not having a place on a specific committee which matters to them, an additional space is sometimes created. This haggling goes on behind the scenes, but is usually concluded without too much fuss.

Once the committee is appointed, the chair (or, where there is no pre-elected chair, the senior member) will write to its members with the date, time and place of a first meeting. As the guide given to new select committee members states: 'The agenda for that meeting will include: declarations of members' interests; setting the time and date of regular meetings; and discussion of the committee's working methods, strategy and consequent forward programme.'[21] Committee membership is a significant time commitment for MPs, with one or two meetings per week, as well as preparation for oral evidence sessions, visits and informal meetings from interest groups.

Committee members are required to declare both the

interests that they are obliged to record in the Register of Members' Financial Interests and any further interests which fall outside of those.

> The non-registered interests might include trusteeships of bodies relevant to the committee's remit or trade union membership; close family connections (for example on the Health Committee a close relative who is a medical professional or on the Defence Committee one who is serving in the Armed Forces); and pecuniary interests which, though not declarable under the House's rules for registration are particularly relevant to the committee's remit.[22]

Due to the rigorous work undertaken by each committee, there have been very few instances at all of members being seen to have inappropriately conducted business without having declared their interests either prior to, or on the day of, a committee session. The transparency of the British system is, I think, to its considerable credit.

GENDER BALANCE

The House of Commons generally has a gender-balance problem, despite improvements in recent times. Of the 650 MPs in Parliament today, 208 are women, which equates to 32 per cent. That is a vast improvement even since the 2010 election, when there were just 143 female MPs, or 22 per cent. There is, however, some way to go.

According to the Institute for Government: 'The Women and Equalities, and Education Committees are the only two committees to have more female than male members. The least balanced committees are Transport and International Development, with just one woman on each – though Transport is chaired by a woman.'[23]

Promisingly, since the 2017 election, several of the most prominent Commons committees have been chaired by women: Nicky Morgan at Treasury; Yvette Cooper at Home Affairs; Rachel Reeves at Business; and Sarah Wollaston at both the Health and Social Care and the Liaison Committees. As the Institute for Government tells us, 'Over one third – nine of the 25 departmental and cross-cutting committees – have female chairs, up from six in the last Parliament.'[24] However, improving these numbers will unfortunately take time, as it ultimately depends on more women being elected to the Commons at each subsequent election.

Parliamentary archivist Dr Mari Takayanagi's PhD thesis, 'Parliament and Women c1900–1945',[25] reveals that there have been female members of select committees since the 1920s. But most select committees during the inter-war period did not have a woman on the panel, at least in part because there were so few female MPs. Those appointed tended to be placed on committees which dealt with what were defined as 'women's' interests – such as the Commons Kitchen Committee (yes, really), or committees on nursing, the guardianship of children, the nationality of married women, or sexual offences. This improved to some extent in the 1930s, when women also appeared on select committees assessing major policy issues, such as Indian Constitutional Reform and Public Petitions.[26]

According to the Institute for Government: 'In the House of Lords, where 25 per cent of active peers are female, women are over-represented as committee members – making up 35 per cent of investigative and ad hoc committee members. However, they are underrepresented among chairs, holding just 19 per cent of available positions.'[27]

MEETINGS

All committees have the right to convene a hearing at any time on any day on which the House itself sits, but in reality most committee sessions take place between Monday and Wednesday, and each committee tends to meet once a week.

Parliament enjoys a number of recesses during which the committees cannot meet to take evidence. In 2016/17, for instance, the UK Parliament sat for 142 days. A general election can cause major disruption to select committees, which we saw especially as a result of the snap election in 2017, when, in some instances, they were out of action between March to early November.

SPLIT REPORTS

If a committee produces a report without the unanimous backing of all its members, it is considered to be a 'split' report. These can be very damaging for the public perception of that committee, but also for internal relations between committee members.

Fortunately they are very rare, but there have been major bust-ups which have led to this outcome. Most recently, you may not be surprised to learn that Brexit has been the cause. The Exiting the European Union (ExEU) Committee was always going to be arguably the most difficult committee to chair in parliamentary history, especially given how the issue has split the entire nation. It is also an unwieldy size, made up of twenty-one MPs, and thus bigger than any other current departmental committee. One current chair told me the number of MPs on the ExEU Committee is a problem, suggesting that it is 'a terrible example of a big committee. Honestly, what has it achieved?'

In April 2018 a row erupted between MPs on the ExEU Committee after publishing a report which said the government should not rule out a Norway-style deal with the EU.[28]

Senior Brexiteer Jacob Rees-Mogg MP said his own committee was trying to 'stop Brexit' and heavily criticised the work of chair Hilary Benn. The report formally split the committee, with Leave-backing MPs voting against the recommendations and against the report in its entirety. 'The ExEU Select Committee report is another effort by Remainers to reverse the result,' he declared. 'Select Committee reports are only of any value when unanimous; divided ones have no effects.'

In a major moment of select committee drama in 2012, the Labour Party deputy leader, Tom Watson, then chair of the Culture, Media and Sport Committee, tabled an amendment to his own committee's report following its questioning of Rupert Murdoch. It accused the News International proprietor of being 'not a fit and proper person to have the stewardship of a major international company'.[29]

The amendment to the report failed to get the support of other members of the committee, in a vote that split along party lines. The move was seen by many to have damaged the committee's credibility and was not considered within its remit, and having met with some of the key people involved at the time, I know it damaged relations between the chair and his members. However, Watson has since argued that members of the committee had been given advance warning that he was proposing the amendment, so should not have claimed that it took them by surprise. Either way, it did undoubtedly taint the otherwise positive reputation of that particular inquiry.

These rare examples of unseemly rows between committee members exemplify the reasons why achieving unanimous backing for a report is essential to maximising its effectiveness and the committee's credibility.

COMMITTEE POWERS

CIVIL SERVANTS

In broad terms, government officials tend to dislike parliamentary scrutiny because it means additional work for them. A select committee hearing featuring one or more of their ministers, or managers in the civil service, can drain many hours in order to marshal the relevant facts and figures, and brief their bosses.

However, beyond the challenges of diaries and resources, there have always been concerns about how civil servants should interact with the select committee shadowing the work of their department. As a result, a guide known as *The Osmotherly Rules* was produced (named after its author, a civil servant called E. B. C. Osmotherly), which is a set of internal guidelines specifying how government departments should provide evidence to select committees.

Although it is said to have 'no formal Parliamentary

standing or approval, nor does it claim to have',[30] the rules cover engagement with both Houses of Parliament.

They were first formally issued in May 1980, although a similar document had been circulating throughout the 1970s. An early edition of the rules was caught up in the Westland affair, a political scandal which famously led to the resignation of Michael Heseltine.

The current edition dates from October 2014 and was issued by the Cabinet Office under the name of 'Giving Evidence to Select Committees'.[31] The rules state that civil servants are not directly accountable to Parliament; rather, government ministers, as the elected agents of the Crown, are accountable to Parliament, and their civil servants (carrying out actions on their behalf) are accountable to them, and thus cannot be summoned by select committees.

The rules cover the occasions on which it is considered appropriate for officials to refrain from giving evidence on the grounds of national security and public interest. The tests in the most recent edition are based on those used by civil servants when considering whether to release material to the public following a freedom of information request.

The rules also provide guidance on other issues, including: the limitations of select committees' powers to 'send for persons, papers and records'; the procedures on committees summoning retired officials; parliamentary privilege; the point at which the cost of supplying information is considered excessive; and the rules of *sub judice*.[32]

PARLIAMENTARY IMMUNITY

The Bill of Rights was the legislation passed by Parliament in December 1689 which formally made law the requirement for a monarch to rule only with the people's consent. A crucial additional strand of the bill stated: 'The freedom of speech and debates or proceedings in Parliament ought not to be impeached or questioned in any court or place out of Parliament.' This means that MPs, while in the environs of the Houses of Parliament, are exempt from libel laws.[33]

This immunity from prosecution applies to speeches, questions or responses given during parliamentary proceedings in the House of Commons and the Lords. However, it does not provide immunity from arrest for criminal charges. Parliamentary privilege is something that forms part of the law, rather than putting members of Parliament above the law. So, if Theresa May finally cracks and thumps Jeremy Corbyn after a testy round of Prime Minister's Questions, she could still be arrested. While outbreaks of sudden violence in advanced democracies may seem unlikely, parliamentary violence is not uncommon around the world. My favourite examples come from South Korea, which has a rich history of fisticuffs. In 2008, opposition MPs used sledgehammers to pound their way into a parliamentary committee room to block the ruling party from introducing a bill to ratify a free trade agreement with the United States.

The other exception to the parliamentary immunity freedoms is anything an MP does outside of the chambers of the House of Commons. The doctrine of parliamentary privilege was unsuccessfully used to try to prevent details of the expenses scandal from emerging. As a result, five former Labour MPs (Elliot Morley, David Chaytor, Eric Illsley, Jim Devine and Denis MacShane) and two Conservative peers (Lord Hanningfield and Lord Taylor) all served prison time for fiddling their office expenses after the extraordinary behaviour of MPs and peers came to light in 2008–09, from which the profession has arguably never really recovered.

Giving Parliament these powers of immunity may seem like yet another perk to protect the powerful, but they make sense when you consider the consequences should they be removed. High-powered lawyers working for either hugely powerful corporations or individuals such as Leave.EU chief Arron Banks would be able to threaten and challenge any parliamentarian who makes an accusation or allegation. Holding these people to account, therefore, would be significantly more challenging and Parliament would lose much of its power and authority. Legal interventions would clog up and slow government policy-making, and damage the chances of attracting good people into politics, given that one false step could mean financial ruin.

Not everyone likes the current system, however. The downside is that MPs can often thumb their noses at due process and make almost any accusation they like, thus subverting the rights of individuals. The esteemed Royal Society of Arts suggested that 'subjecting people, however powerful, to a courtroom style cross-examination without proper procedure or protections borders on the unjust and possibly a departure from due process'.[34]

This issue became a hot topic again in 2018 when Labour peer Peter Hain used the powers of immunity to name Sir Philip Green as the high-profile boss who had used a super-injunction to prevent allegations of sexual harassment being published by the *Daily Telegraph*. The initial praise Hain received for being the first to name the business leader was quickly replaced by concern about whether it represented justice and British values.

As previously stated, when gathering evidence, almost all select committees have the power to send for 'persons, papers and records'. This means that committees can insist upon the attendance of witnesses and the production of papers and other material. Further, when hearing oral evidence, committees have the power to compel witnesses to answer questions. However, in practice, evidence-taking before committees is conducted with a degree of informality and such powers are seldom used. A committee can also take evidence on oath. If the procedure is used, which it has been on extremely rare occasions, witnesses are liable to the laws of perjury.

Witnesses to select committees also enjoy absolute privilege in respect of the evidence they give, whether written or oral, provided that it is formally accepted as such by the committee. In practical terms, this means that witnesses are immune from civil or criminal proceedings founded upon that evidence, and their evidence cannot be relied upon in civil or criminal proceedings against any other person. Absolute privilege does not apply to written submissions which have been distributed or made available prior to being published by a committee. As Parliament's own 'Guide for Witnesses' states, the protection which absolute privilege gives to those preparing written evidence and to witnesses 'must not be abused'. In particular, 'Witnesses should answer questions put to them by a committee carefully, fully and honestly. Deliberately attempting to mislead a Committee is a contempt of the House.'[35]

In reality – certainly with the companies and individuals with whom I have worked – witnesses always tend to err on the side of caution with any issue which has legal sensitivity, regardless of the protections provided. They also tend to seek advance assurances from the committee that they will not be expected to publicly offer up information that is commercially sensitive.

PUBLIC PROFILE

MEDIA COVERAGE

The media is always looking for a good story, and in the realm of politics a bruising select committee hearing can really play into its hands. In all public select committee hearings, journalists are assigned seats so they can ensure the sessions are covered, but with the advent of ParliamentLive (more on that shortly) the media no longer has to physically be there. For TV media, some select committee sessions are broadcast on Parliament TV, but often rolling news channels will cover them too – especially those which have made national news. The evening bulletins will also use clips of any particularly gruelling session as part of their daily review.

A committee will ordinarily conclude an inquiry by agreeing a report to the House. It may decide to issue embargoed copies of the report to the media up to seventy-two hours in advance of publication; this provides a great opportunity for journalists to write up their stories ready for the release of the formal report. Committees also occasionally hold press conferences to coincide with report publication. As well as journalists, witnesses can attend, as can other members of the public.

Perhaps unsurprisingly, the media tends to care about a select committee hearing, or subsequent report, when it fits with a wider political news story. For example, when the then Labour government was embroiled in a bitter battle with the BBC over a new piece which claimed the Prime Minister had 'sexed up' its dossier in advance of the invasion of Iraq in 2003, the subsequent select committee hearing featuring the journalist's source, Dr David Kelly, became disproportionately important to the development of the story.[36]

More recent select committees have also piqued the interest of the media. Whether it is self-proclaimed 'Brexit bad boy' Arron Banks walking out of his Digital, Culture, Media and Sport Committee hearing mid-questioning, with the chair looking on aghast, or Amber Rudd and David Davis coming unstuck during their sessions, there are moments when select committees can be front and centre of the news cycle.

However, one senior radio and political journalist I spoke with told me that, generally speaking, select committees are not held in high regard by his profession. He said that the general quality of questioning of ministers by MPs is not nearly as rigorous as that of journalists, so unless the report chimes with a blockbuster story, it is unlikely to get significant coverage on broadcast news channels. This may be, in his view, part of the reason why select committees have increasingly moved away from their remit to shadow the work of government, and instead begun to target high-profile business leaders. By broadening the media scope away from so-called 'lobby' journalists and towards those who cover business, it increases the chances of attracting interest.

PARLIAMENTLIVE

ParliamentLive.tv is the online portal that allows anyone with an internet or phone connection to watch parliamentary activities, either live or on demand. It can be watched on desktop, mobile and tablet and is supported on most up-to-date browsers, and has video and audio footage of all UK Parliament events that take place in public.[37]

It also covers debates and chamber proceedings from both the House of Commons and the House of Lords, as well as all select committees. It has an archive which goes back to 4 December 2007, so many of the major committee moments I reference in this book can be watched back. You can use the search function on the top right of the home-page to find an event by name, member, the House it took place in, or date.

According to the website, you can get an email with a link to a section of the video or audio footage you want. To do this, go to the event you are interested in and select the start and end times of the section you want to download.

The viewing figures are not a matter of public record, but committee sources I have spoken with suggest that thousands of people watch some of the higher-profile sessions, with numbers dwindling as the sessions become more obscure in topic.

COMMITTEES ON TOUR

A growing feature of parliamentary select committee hearings has been to take them out of Westminster entirely and into the UK regions, and in one recent instance, out of the country entirely.

As with the push for regional select committees under Gordon Brown's Labour government, taking committees to different regions has been seen by some as a PR stunt, by demonstrating that there is a world beyond Westminster and using it as an opportunity to be seen to engage a wider audience. A similar thing has happened with Cabinet meetings being held outside of London by both the Labour and Conservative governments.[38] Unfortunately, as one interviewee caustically said to me, 'finding out that an obscure parliamentary select committee is in your town probably won't be enough to convince you to pull a sickie at work'.

That said, in some instances a regional hearing makes perfect sense. For example, if you were conducting an inquiry into the impact of cutting bus services in the north-west, it would be helpful to host at least some of the oral evidence in Manchester, Liverpool or Warrington, rather than hauling all the relevant people down to London.

One select committee took this much, much further. In February 2018, Damian Collins, chair of the Digital, Culture, Media and Sport Committee, decided to take his group of MPs to the United States as part of his inquiry into fake news. In order to secure the most senior possible witnesses from the major tech firms, Collins announced that a number of hearings would be held in Washington, DC, with additional site visits in New York. Needless to say, this drew some ire from the cynical UK political media, always on the search for post-expenses scandal examples of public money being wasted. The total cost was confirmed by the committee as amounting to £84,000.[39] Collins, however, remained unapologetic, and a statement published on the Digital, Culture, Media and Sport Committee website justified the trip by saying that fake news and the spread of misinformation was 'one of the most serious threats facing our democracy today'.[40]

An investigative piece by Politico revealed: 'Eleven MPs and three officials travelled to the United States in February to meet social media executives at a cost of £69,535 to the taxpayer. A further £14,655 was spent broadcasting an evidence session from George Washington University … according to figures released under Freedom of Information rules.' The committee held meetings with the *New York Times*, Google and NowThis Media in New York, as well as Senators Richard Burr and Mark Warner, who serve on the Intelligence Committee, and were given a tour of Congress.

Collins later had to deny claims that the US tech companies being examined had offered to pay for the committee's flights, but said that they had 'all agreed that it would be easier to get people to come and give evidence if we held a session in America'. He said the visit would help the committee to present the most informed policy recommendations and solutions to government when producing its report.

The cost of this visit was approved in the normal method

by the Liaison Committee, who sign off all select committee visits – just as they did with the other select
committees who also visited the United States recently.
Because of the nature of the topic we're tackling, transparency, truth and communication, we broke with normal
practice of select committee visits and decided to live
broadcast the session so that people around the world
could engage with its contents. In fact, these social media
and tech companies rarely come up against such public
scrutiny. It was always agreed with these companies that
they would provide witnesses to give evidence in the
United States.[41]

My suspicion is that the backlash against this particular
trip makes it unlikely that a select committee hearing will
take place on foreign soil again for a very long time. It is,
of course, perfectly reasonable that select committees occasionally organise short working visits overseas where they
are directly relevant to increasing the knowledge of the
committee's members. One chair expressed sympathy for
Collins's decision: 'We get criticised for creating overseas
visits as part of our inquiries, but they are very valuable in
both getting an understanding of an issue and also publicis-
ing select committee work around the world.'

I do accept that it is difficult to see how the Foreign Affairs Committee, for example, could avoid such visits as part
of enlarging their understanding of the issues they examine.
However, it is much more justifiable for most committees to
hold a hearing in Wigan rather than Washington.

MEMORABLE CHAIRS

Being a select committee chair is a big opportunity to become a significant political figure and secure a place in parliamentary history. Often, the select committees that are considered most effective are successful as a result of the drive, determination and personality of their chairs. Those committees which hog the most headlines do so largely because their chairs are seen to hold powerful people to account. This is why a committee doing broadly the same set of activities and examining similar issues, but which is led by a quieter chair, can seem to disappear from view. For example, the Labour chair of the Public Accounts Committee, Meg Hillier, has not made much of a splash since she took over the role in 2015, despite being a very tenacious and capable parliamentarian. Her predecessor, Margaret Hodge, was barely out of the headlines for five years because she had an innate talent for understanding populist issues and wielded the committee's powers like a baseball bat.

Having closely examined those who have been viewed as particularly successful in the role, the characteristics of being a top chair include the ability to:

- gain the respect of committee members across party divides;
- spot the right policy issues at the right time and to act quickly to seize the agenda;
- spot flaws in a witness's oral evidence and be willing (and able) to change direction;
- deliver a withering put-down or soundbite;
- attract media attention for the committee's work; and
- produce reports that have a direct impact on government policy.

I have looked through the rich history of modern select committees, and identified some of the very best chairs who have extolled some, or in some cases all, of these virtues.

GWYNETH DUNWOODY (CHAIR, TRANSPORT COMMITTEE 1997–2008)

Before the Wright Reforms and the rise of the maverick chairs we have seen under the new system, Labour MP Gwyneth Dunwoody was the most feared parliamentary select committee figurehead of her generation.

Her career was one which came to fruition only in her later years in Parliament. There was no role for her on her party's shadow front bench in the early 1990s, so she took up a role on the Speaker's panel, from which select committee chairs were then drawn. Dunwoody eventually took on the transport sub-committee of the wider group on Environment, Transport and Rural Affairs (ETRA). Little did anyone realise just how brilliantly she would take advantage of this seeming backwater of parliamentary scrutiny.

In 1997, the year Tony Blair was elected as the first Labour Prime Minister since 1979, she was appointed chair of that ETRA committee, overseeing the ministerial work of John Prescott. She had a talented committee, but most importantly she was a powerful and charismatic chair.

She was a nightmare to face from the other side of the committee room, and was labelled 'the queen of the withering put-downs of puffed-up witnesses'. She herself observed: 'Awkward old bats have their purpose.'[42] A classic example is this exchange between Dunwoody and Rosie Winterton, then a middle-ranking Transport minister, who was giving evidence on the cost of the European Galileo project.

> Chair: Could I also ask you, Minister, because, although we did have a very clear statement of the government's position, it was a rather gentle glide over vulgar things like the figures involved, could you be frightfully working class and go back and find out what the actual money is we are talking about?
>
> Winterton: The Commission itself has said it believes that the cost has increased by … it is asking for another £1.67 billion (€2.4 billion).
>
> Chair: Is that on top of the £5.1 billion that was the original estimate?
>
> Winterton: No, it is not. The costs so far have been £1.1 billion. I am doing this in pounds, by the way.

Chair: Oh, good, what a clever lady. You will obviously
have a long career.[43]

Cue gales of inappropriate laughter in the committee room.

Arguably her greatest success was in highlighting the
issues related to the privatisation of rail in the UK and the
separation of track maintenance from the provision of route
services. She was saying many years prior to the collapse of
Railtrack in 2001 that it was doomed to fail, despite angry
protestations from government ministers who came before
her in the committee room. This made her exceedingly
popular with many Labour colleagues, who felt uncomfortable with their party's move to the centre-right on certain
policies, as well as with rail commuters, who could see no
improvement to the passenger experience, as had been
promised.

Her combative style ensured that the media paid particular attention to her sessions, meaning that transport issues
received a disproportionate amount of coverage during her
time as chair. Combined with her general outspokenness on
the wider policies of the New Labour government, she made
an enemy of the Labour whips.

It was perhaps no surprise when, after the 2001 general
election, she and Donald Anderson, who had chaired the
Foreign Affairs Committee, were both ruthlessly removed
from their committees. However, the furious response to
this widely condemned example of petty party management
took the government by surprise. Prime Minister Blair
made a sharp and undignified retreat and Dunwoody never

looked back.[44] She became even more powerful and continued to hold the government to account until her untimely death in 2008. I think it is very telling that the Transport Committee has never since had such a strong public profile.

ANDREW TYRIE (CHAIR, TREASURY COMMITTEE 2010–2017)

When Tyrie stepped down as both an MP and chair of the powerful Treasury Committee before the 2017 general election, he left with huge respect from all political sides for his chairmanship. He was described by Donald Macintyre of *The Independent* in 2013 as 'the most powerful backbencher in the House of Commons'.[45]

From conversations I have had with his political contemporaries over the years, he was not, however, hugely popular amongst some of his Conservative colleagues. One told me that 'his general reputation for being a loner was possibly the reason why he never made it to high office'. The *Financial Times* speculated in 2012: 'One possible reason why Mr Tyrie is still on the backbenches is that he irritated David Cameron by challenging his climate change policies. Mr Cameron did not ask him to become a Minister after the 2010 election and his nickname in senior Tory circles is "Andrew Tiresome."'[46]

He was first elected as MP for Chichester in 1997, having previously served as a special advisor at the Treasury. He took up his role as committee chair in June 2010, having defeated original favourite Michael Fallon (later Defence

Secretary), and returned unopposed after the 2015 general election. In January 2016, Tyrie clashed with David Cameron over the Prime Minister's refusal to release details related to the UK's involvement in Syria. At one especially heated moment, Cameron exclaimed to Tyrie: 'You don't know what you're talking about.' Tyrie's questioning during the January 2016 session of the committee was described in *The Guardian* as a 'one-man opposition'.[47]

When the snap election was called in 2017 by Theresa May, he decided to stand down as both an MP and chair of the committee. In April 2018, Tyrie was named as the next chair of the important regulator the Competition and Markets Authority, and shortly afterwards was made a member of the House of Lords. He is already making mischief in his new role, triggering a major study into the so-called Big Four audit firms.

MARGARET HODGE (CHAIR, PUBLIC ACCOUNTS COMMITTEE 2010–2015)

If you were to poll members of the public (who have actually heard of a select committee) to name a chair past or present, the most likely name to emerge would be Margaret Hodge. One chair told me that Hodge, 'with her combative approach, was a good thing for the select committee system. People started talking about our impact in the media.'

Regardless of how you view her, it cannot be denied that she made an extraordinary success of her position heading the PAC for the five years of coalition government. Hodge was elected as chair of the PAC in June 2010 after five rounds of voting, and she never looked back.

Her enemies claimed that she went against established practice in order to hold civil servants to account. She had a famous public spat with Gus O'Donnell, then head of the Civil Service, who accused her of presiding over a 'theatrical exercise in public humiliation'.[48]

However, it was her work attacking tech giants, payday lenders, tax consultants and outsourcers, amongst others, that made her a figure of supreme terror in boardrooms.

Despite having previously served as both the leader of a major London borough and a government minister, she said she felt she had more influence as a committee chair than she did when serving in a department. According to the BBC, 'between June 2013 and June 2014, she was mentioned nearly 2,000 times in the press, more than many government ministers'.[49]

Amusingly, Hodge never denied her critics' attacks that she failed to respect convention. Peter Riddell, writing for the Institute for Government, assessed her position based upon a speech she gave in 2012 to think tank Policy Exchange:

> In her view, the old doctrine of accountability is not fit for the 21st century since it lets both ministers and civil servants off the hook. 'Politicians resent having to accept responsibility for mistakes made by civil servants and civil servants resent being blamed without being able to

clear their names'. And there is the further twist in an age of payment by results and performance management, that 'ministers are prevented from themselves appointing, promoting or sacking the senior civil servants for whom they are said to be accountable, on the grounds that this would politicise the civil service'.[50]

Although she terrified multinationals accused of dodging their fair share of taxes, she did face significant criticism herself when Helia Ebrahimi, former City correspondent of the *Telegraph*, raised the issue of her supposed hypocrisy, reporting that Hodge's family company 'pays just 0.01pc tax on £2.1bn of business generated in the UK'.[51] Hodge made clear that she was not responsible for the running of the scheme, and paid all the taxes due on her shareholding.

Shortly after the 2015 general election, Hodge announced she would not be standing for re-election to the PAC, much to the delight of CEOs across the UK. She said:

> I've done the job for five years and it has been really hard work but fantastically rewarding. I've really loved it. I am hugely proud of the work we did as a committee, and a new chair will bring a fresh approach that I'm sure will see it continue to go from strength to strength.[52]

Hodge has since written an entertaining book about her time as chair of the PAC entitled *Called to Account*.

KEITH VAZ (CHAIR, HOME AFFAIRS COMMITTEE 2007–2016)

Keith Vaz has been the Labour MP for Leicester East since 1987, and is Parliament's longest-serving British Asian MP. Never far from controversy, he undoubtedly created a high profile for himself and his committee. His style could be at least as gruelling as a session with Margaret Hodge, and he was widely regarded as the chair most likely to instigate knee-jerk inquiry sessions as a result of a topical news story. As one current committee official told me, 'Keith used to decide his inquiries based upon whatever was in the papers that morning.' Sometimes, such as during the hearing regarding outsourcer G4S's failure to hire sufficient security for the London 2012 Olympics, he was able to help ruthlessly dispatch senior executives.

Prior to joining the select committee circuit, he was a minister during Tony Blair's first term in office, but suffered a number of scandals which forced his resignation and damaged his reputation.

He was chair of the Home Affairs Committee from July 2007, replacing the respected John Denham, albeit having been selected in an unconventional way. He was the only nomination brought forward by the then Leader of the House, Harriet Harman, who claimed there was not sufficient time to go through the usual procedure for appointing a chair before the impending summer recess. It was suspected to have been a stitch-up. It could be argued that, had he sought to become a first-time chair after the 2009

Wright Reforms, he may well have failed. As it was, he was re-elected in 2015 – incumbency becomes a position of great strength for a committee chair.

The former Conservative MP Patrick Mercer was recorded by a hidden camera as describing Vaz as 'a crook of the first order', adding that he had 'never met an operator like him ... I mean it's not always completely ethical but it's stunning, he is an operator.'[53]

Vaz later resigned after serving nine years in the chair after he was entrapped by the *Sunday Mirror* with a tawdry story involving male prostitutes, cocaine and washing machines.[54]

Just a month after resigning from his own committee, he brazenly reappeared as a member of the Justice Committee; a parliamentary vote to block this move was defeated.

DAMIAN COLLINS (CHAIR, DIGITAL, CULTURE, MEDIA AND SPORT COMMITTEE 2016–PRESENT)

Of the more recent select committee chairs, Damian Collins continues to be the one to watch. He has been the MP for Kent constituency Folkestone and Hythe since 2010.

He is a former advertising executive at M&C Saatchi, having previously worked in the Conservative Research Department. Prior to becoming an MP, he was a senior advisor at a communications firm for companies such as British Airways. In May 2006, Collins was included on the so-called A-list of Conservative parliamentary candidates, created by David Cameron.

In July 2010 he was elected as a member of the Culture,

Media and Sport committee, which he now chairs. Due to the rules which permit a non-paid ministerial aide to continue to serve on a select committee, Collins also made the first rung of junior ministerial life in 2012, as Parliamentary Private Secretary to the Secretary of State for Northern Ireland.

Since he was elected chair in 2016, Collins has arguably scored more hits than most of his fellow chairs and has attracted huge publicity for his work. In particular, he has helped to uncover corruption at football governing body FIFA; exposed prejudice within English women's football; conducted a major inquiry into fake news which has included attempts to snare Facebook's founder Mark Zuckerberg and Cambridge Analytica's Alexander Nix; challenged the BBC on star pay; and had major bust-ups with Vote Leave luminaries such as Dominic Cummings and Arron Banks.

Collins, arguably more than almost any chair in recent times, has also pulled and tugged at the conventions and powers afforded to select committees. It has not necessarily always worked (and has annoyed some other chairs in the process, judging by my interviews), but he has at least prompted a whole debate about whether the powers of select committees are now fit for purpose (an issue which I explore in Part 2 of this book).

GREATEST HITS

ANDREW CECIL, DIRECTOR OF EU PUBLIC POLICY, AMAZON (NOVEMBER 2012)

BACKGROUND

As the internet emerged from nowhere, becoming interwoven into every aspect of our daily lives, technology companies were largely seen as a force for societal good. The innovation in tech services was combined with a public image which seemed friendly, soft and cool. Governments around the world, including ours here in Britain, embraced them in a desperate attempt to persuade them to invest in the UK and help to deliver more efficient public services through technological solutions.

The problem is that most of these technology companies (and other multinationals) were unfortunately engaged in that most traditional and uncool activity, doing all they could within the law to minimise their tax bills. This behaviour was not public knowledge until the financial crisis of 2007–08 caused widespread economic harm, and increased the gap between the haves and have nots in society. Given that we were suddenly living in an age of austerity, with public services cut and taxes rising, it suddenly became apparent that multinational companies were not just run in a tax-efficient way, but were creating and inventing a whole range of clever tricks to evade taxes which would otherwise help fund schools, hospitals and elements of our civic life.

WHAT HAPPENED?

PAC chair Margaret Hodge had been reading the investigative work of the Reuters journalist Tom Bergin, who has exposed some of the extraordinary lengths companies were going to in order to avoid paying national taxes.[55] Hodge decided to call in a number of the most high-profile companies to hear from them directly.

However, the November 2012 exposé of the so-called 'tax-dodging three' – Amazon, Starbucks and Google – almost did not happen. Margaret Hodge's initial intention was to only take evidence from the US coffee giant Starbucks. However, by chance they succeeded in a speculative attempt to get Google, who sent in senior executive Matt Brittin, and Amazon, who sent director of public policy for Europe Andrew Cecil.

Where do I begin? I would describe the three witnesses as the good, the bad and the ugly. Google, as one of the members on that committee admitted to me, did a good job holding firm on its corporate position. It may not have entirely washed with the viewing public, but Brittin was a smart witness, able to dodge and ride many of the punches.

For Starbucks it was bad. Troy Alstead, its chief operating officer, was rather too open with the committee and gave evidence which was far too interesting, along the way admitting that the company had a special tax deal with the Dutch government in return for basing its European HQ there. This triggered long-lasting reputational damage for the company, with an initial hit on its store footfall in the UK and an unprecedented move to make a prepayment of tax to the UK authorities.[56] For Alstead, there were personal consequences – he had been considered a possible future CEO of the company, but he left after the tax row had exploded.[57]

Amazon were the ugly. For most Westminster watchers, the oral evidence provided by Andrew Cecil is the worst select committee evidence ever provided, and to this day I can only watch it from behind a sofa.[58] The select committee had originally asked for the boss of Amazon's UK business, Christopher North, but he wisely found a reason not to attend and let a policy wonk within the business appear instead. Cecil was unfortunately a lamb to the slaughter.

For many, this hearing is the best example of how a select committee can jolt the public consciousness of a policy issue and effect change, more so than blockbuster sessions featuring giants of the business world, such as Rupert Murdoch or Philip Green. This is because the witnesses went in to the session believing that hiding behind the law would be enough to deflect criticism. When exposed to the court of public opinion, all three were declared guilty.

The impact on these three companies obviously differed massively. For Amazon and Google, with their market dominance, the impacts were mainly reputational. They both continue to hurtle on as multi-billion-pound companies, although it triggered a discussion for the first time about their social purpose in the world. For Starbucks, the impact was financially greater. After all, coffee can be purchased almost anywhere today, and so customers can vote with their feet. You can link many of the current criticisms of those companies to this debate around tax, which was brought to prominence by the PAC.

KEY EXCHANGES

I have included here a long exchange from the session to demonstrate how a select committee hearing can build to a crescendo. At this point in an already heated debate, Conservative MP Steve Barclay is trying to understand why Amazon EU claims to be a company based in Luxembourg when, as a UK customer, we might assume that we are transacting with a company based here and which is therefore liable for local corporation taxes. The other MPs who get involved in this exchange are the chair, Margaret Hodge, Labour's Nick Smith MP, Lib Dem Ian Swales MP and Conservative Richard Bacon MP.[59]

Stephen Barclay: Who owns the Luxembourg company?

Andrew Cecil: Luxembourg is owned by a holding company, which is a subsidiary of our group companies.

Stephen Barclay: Where is that located?

Andrew Cecil: The holding company is also in Luxembourg.

Stephen Barclay: It is also in Luxembourg. That seems a slightly artificial arrangement, doesn't it?

Andrew Cecil: I am not familiar with the details of the holding company, but I would be very happy to come back to the committee.

Stephen Barclay: So what is the effective tax rate that you
pay in Luxembourg?

Andrew Cecil: Worldwide – I have the figures here—

Stephen Barclay: No, in Luxembourg.

Andrew Cecil: I would need a calculator. I apologise. For
2011, our net profit after tax was €20 million, on revenues of €9.1 billion.

Stephen Barclay: Sorry, can you just say that again? In
Luxembourg, your profit was €20 million.

Andrew Cecil: Our revenues across Europe for 2011 for
Amazon EU Sarl were €9.1 billion. Our profit after tax
was €20 million. The tax expense—

Nick Smith: Did you say that your profit after tax was €20
million?

Andrew Cecil: Maybe to that point, I would point out
that we are investing very significantly not just in the
UK but across Europe, which may be reflected in these
numbers.

Stephen Barclay: Do you have preferred equity certifi-
cates, then, in Luxembourg?

Andrew Cecil: I wouldn't know. I am very happy to find
out and come back to you. Maybe I can finish on the
point that the tax we paid – and this is a tax expense
recorded on our accounts for 2011—

Stephen Barclay: What I am interested in is how you are
stripping out the profits in Luxembourg, because that
is the impression. If it is €9.1 billion going to €20 million that suggests that you are stripping out the profit
in Luxembourg. Who owns the holding company?

Andrew Cecil: I will need to come back to the committee on that.

Stephen Barclay: So the profit is going into a company, and is then going to a holding company. What about the title and goods from affiliates or third parties—

Ian Swales: Sorry, that is another unacceptable answer. You are telling us you don't know the corporate structure of your company. Really?

Andrew Cecil: I do know the corporate structure of the European company. I work for the European company. I would be happy to come back.

Ian Swales: All we need to know is who owns the holding company.

Richard Bacon: You are the director of public policy. It is incredible that you wouldn't know who owns the holding company. It is just not credible.

Andrew Cecil: I am very happy to come back to the committee.

Richard Bacon: Well, you can tell that we are not happy.

Chair: Do you know who owns it?

Andrew Cecil: No. I will come back to the committee with an answer.

Chair: Do you know who owns it?

Andrew Cecil: No, I personally do not know—

Chair: Do you know who owns it?

Andrew Cecil: No, I don't.

Stephen Barclay: But it is where the money goes, isn't it?

Chair: Isn't there someone behind you? Haven't you brought advisors with you?

Stephen Barclay: Well, we have probably got another forty minutes or an hour to go. I am sure one of your advisors could go and make a call, and come back to us in ten or fifteen minutes, with the chair's permission, with the answer. It can't be too difficult to phone head office and find out who owns it, can it, Mr Cecil?

Andrew Cecil: I will certainly provide that information to the committee.

Stephen Barclay: So we can have that before we close today? That would be useful. What I am interested in, really, is where the profit is going and how it has been stripped out. Can we look at it in a different way, through title and goods from third parties and affiliates – can you talk through how that is handled?

Andrew Cecil: Again, I am not quite sure what you are specifically talking about. It is very clear what our revenues are, what our profits are and what tax expense we have accounted for across Europe. The inventory of goods that are in our fulfilment centres across Europe belongs to Amazon EU Sarl and does not belong to the local entities that we may have across Europe.

Stephen Barclay: So why is the UK not a branch?

Andrew Cecil: I am not a detailed tax expert on that question, but again I would be very happy to come back to you.

Stephen Barclay: Because it is a tax issue – it is not a business issue. It is about getting the structure of the tax bill.

Nick Smith: Let me ask this question again. Of the €9.1 billion of European sales in 2011, what were your sales in the UK in 2011?

Andrew Cecil: If I may, I will give the same reply to the committee – I will come back to the committee and if it is possible to disclose that figure I will disclose it.

Mr Bacon: Could you say that again?

Andrew Cecil: I will come back to the committee. I will see whether it is possible to disclose that figure. We have not disclosed those figures, ever, publicly, either on a country basis or a website basis.

Stephen Barclay: Why is it so confidential what your earnings are by country? I might be missing something, being a generalist, but what is the secret that pertains to country-by-country data?

Andrew Cecil: This is how we have disclosed our financial data over a number of years now. We have never broken out revenues on a country basis.

Chair: What are you hiding?

Andrew Cecil: We are not hiding anything, chair. As I said, I am very happy to come back to the chair on a confidential basis and see whether it is possible to disclose that.

Nick Smith: That, Mr Cecil, is the most ridiculous answer I have heard in months and months on this committee. That is just pathetic. Of the €9.1 billion sales you made in 2011, you have said that you made €20 million after tax. What did you make before tax?

Andrew Cecil: I would assume – again, I don't have the figures – that, as we had a tax expense that was around €8 million, that we made a profit of the two combined. But I would need to check.

Nick Smith: So you made a profit of €30 million on revenue of €9 billion? Is that what you are saying?

Andrew Cecil: No, what I am saying is we made an after-tax profit of €20 million on that specifically.

Nick Smith: What was your profit before tax?

Andrew Cecil: Before tax – I do not have that specific number there, but I am happy to provide it to the committee.

Chair: Mr Cecil, you don't have anything. Honestly, you have come to us with absolutely no information. What is your job?

Andrew Cecil: I am director of public policy for Amazon across Europe.

Chair: Well, I think what we are going to have to do is order somebody to come who can give us answers to the questions we ask. We will order somebody to appear before us who does that. It is just not acceptable. I don't know what you take us for, but we need proper answers to perfectly proper questions, which are trying to establish the economic activity in this country, and therefore what would be a reasonable corporation tax due. That is our job. The idea that you come here and simply do not answer the questions, and pretend ignorance, is just not on. It is awful.

Andrew Cecil: Chair, I am very happy to provide the committee with any responses to these questions.

Chair: No. I cannot believe you have come without the information – or they have deliberately sent you. We will order somebody who can answer the questions, in public.

CONCLUSION

OK, so Amazon's business has relentlessly grown in the UK regardless of this select committee inquiry and the subsequent fall-out played out in the media and politics, but you have to be mindful that, prior to this point, Amazon was seen as a force for good. The UK government saw the company as a potential provider of huge numbers of jobs, and to build regional sites which could help struggling local economies. We have reached a point where measuring a company solely by its revenue growth alone is not enough, and this hearing was one of the key moments in arriving at that conclusion. The company's reputation in the UK and across Europe has been tainted for ever.

You might say that Andrew Cecil was on a hiding to nothing. He was always going to be confronted with a narrative on a tax policy which he did not decide, and he could never have realistically won in a debate with deeply suspicious and cynical MPs.

However, it is inconceivable that Amazon could not have anticipated this series of questions. If they did not, it is a shameful reflection of their lack of judgement at the time. They should have put forward a genuine expert on their tax structures. Poor Andrew Cecil was clearly working without the proper facts, and it did not just damage his personal reputation, but also that of the wider company. Either the witness really didn't understand his own business (in which case, why bother sending him?), or he did know but pretended not to.

The number of times he was forced to admit to the committee that he did not have the information they required was humiliating.

NICK BUCKLES, CHIEF EXECUTIVE, G4S (JULY 2012)

BACKGROUND

G4S, a private outsourcing and security company based in the UK, is one of the largest companies in the world, operating in over ninety countries and employs 570,000 people. At the time it announced it was signing a £284 million contract to provide security services at the London 2012 Olympic Games, it was a hugely successful company which had grown quietly and largely away from the public eye.

G4S was due to provide 10,400 members of staff to help the organisers cope with the influx of Olympic visitors, but there were immediately serious concerns about the training and accountability of G4S employees.

Less than a month before the opening ceremony, G4S announced that it would not be able to fully provide the staff it had said it would, a shortfall of over 3,500 staff. Even people who had accepted jobs with G4S reported to the BBC that they were dumbfounded by a lack of contact with the company, and many of them had not turned up to their shifts.[60]

Given the short notice, the armed forces had to be called in to fill the spaces, meaning that over 17,000 military personnel would be on the ground or on standby in London during the games, with these well-trained troops being used for menial tasks. According to confidential documents obtained later by the *Daily Telegraph*: 'G4S's management fee rose from £7.3 million to £60 million. Almost £34 million of the increase was for the G4S "programme management office" overseeing the security operation, compared to an increase of just £2.8 million in the firm's recruitment spending."[61]

WHAT HAPPENED?

Although the London 2012 Games are now considered a huge success, there was a string of stories at the time which suggested that the country had not adequately prepared. In the midst of this shambolic episode, Keith Vaz, the publicity-hungry chair of the Home Affairs Committee spied an opportunity and hauled in the company's chief executive, Nick Buckles, to face the music.

Buckles was a dream candidate for this grilling. He was not the typical chief executive of such a huge global company. A former Essex postman with wonderfully coiffured hair and a self-proclaimed fan of Margaret Thatcher, Buckles had led the company since 2005 and had been well remunerated in the process. I later learned from a company insider that Buckles had resisted a major programme of formal select committee training offered by his team, and so walked into a firestorm.

The hearing was featured on a range of broadcast news channels and became a wider political story. Mr Buckles resigned just months later.[62]

KEY EXCHANGES

Here, the committee is seeking to score an early win during the session by attempting to get Nick Buckles to admit to G4S's shambolic handling of the security arrangements. The chair, Labour MP David Winnick (one of the toughest select committee questioners of recent years), seeks a quote from the CEO which the committee knows will form the subsequent media analysis.[63]

The other witness from G4S was Ian Horseman-Sewell, then the managing director for global events at G4S. He resigned shortly afterwards.[64]

> David Winnick: Many would take the view that the reputation of the company is now in tatters. You wouldn't agree.
>
> Nick Buckles: I think at the moment, I would have to agree with you. We have had a fantastic track record of service delivery over many years in many countries, but clearly this is not a good position to be in, but we feel that we have to make every endeavour to deliver as well as we can on this contract.
>
> David Winnick: Mr Buckles, it is a humiliating shambles, isn't it?
>
> Nick Buckles: It is not where we would want to be, that is certain.
>
> David Winnick: It is a humiliating shambles for the company, yes or no?
>
> Nick Buckles: I cannot disagree with you.
>
> David Winnick: No, I would not have thought you would.

• • •

Although the G4S witnesses had seemed suitably contrite and apologetic during the session, the chair Keith Vaz uncovered the fact that the company planned to continue to collect a management fee for the contract. This played into the chair's hands, and he was able to strike.

> Chair: What I cannot understand is why you do not just waive the whole fee on this contract. Bearing in mind what has happened, why are you claiming any money at all?
>
> Nick Buckles: Because we have had management in place for two years to plan the contract and we will have management on venues to help run the venues.
>
> Chair: We understand that, but clearly what was going to be your profit? You talk about loss now, and you said, I think it was to Sky Television, £30 million to £50 million. It is quite a big gap between £30 million and £50 million.
>
> Nick Buckles: Yes.
>
> Chair: What was your profit on the original contract?
>
> Nick Buckles: £10 million.
>
> Chair: So that profit has gone?
>
> Nick Buckles: Correct.
>
> Chair: So bearing in mind all these changes, are you still going to claim your management fee at all?
>
> Nick Buckles: Yes.
>
> Chair: Why? You have not managed.
>
> Nick Buckles: Because we have managed the contract and will have management on the ground.
>
> Chair: But even after all that has happened, you still wish to claim the management fee?

Nick Buckles: Yes.

Chair: How much is it?

Nick Buckles: I do not know.

Chair: Well, how do you know you want to claim it then?

Nick Buckles: In principle, it is part of the contract that we have been providing for the last 18 months.

Chair: Yes, but if you do not know what the management fee is, why do you want to claim it? You have told us what the profit was – £10 million.

Nick Buckles: Yes.

Chair: So what is the management fee?

Ian Horseman-Sewell: The total management fee on the current budgets with our client is in the order of £57 million.

Chair: £57 million is your fee? You still think you ought to claim it?

Nick Buckles: Yes.

Chair: Even after all that has happened?

Nick Buckles: We still expect to deliver a significant number of staff for the Olympics.

Chair: I find that astonishing.

• • •

In summing up the session, the chair tries his luck again in generating a strong set of headlines for the media. Having got the company to accept it had messed up, yet was still claiming a fee, he finished with an attempt to make Buckles comment on his future as CEO.

Chair: I have to say, I asked the members of the committee to sum up your performance and the performance of the company so far, and they have used these terms, 'Unacceptable, incompetent and amateurish'. Though the committee is most grateful to you for coming in, we feel that those words best express our deep concern about the way in which this matter has been handled.

As for you, Mr Horseman-Sewell, I think it was irresponsible to make a statement on 6 July stating you could manage to deliver the Olympics in Australia and London on the same day, when you knew that there were concerns about the way in which this contract has been delivered. In the end, Mr Buckles, it is a matter for you to decide what you do about your future.

Nick Buckles: I agree.

Chair: But this committee will continue to monitor very carefully what happens over the next weeks and we want to ensure that you are able to deliver, with the police and the military, the best Games the world has ever seen.

Nick Buckles: Agreed.

Chair: Then of course it is for you to decide what you want to do about your future.

Nick Buckles: Agreed.

CONCLUSION

The committee played a very cynical game in this hearing, but it achieved its goals. The media coverage of the session was huge, with footage broadcast across news channels – a feat which select committees usually struggle to achieve.

The strategy of the MPs was to skewer the witness on three levels. Firstly, to get them to accept wrongdoing, but in the language of their choosing. Buckles did not actually utter the words 'in tatters' and 'humiliating shambles', but because he agreed with the line of questioning from David Winnick, the media were able to report it that way.

Secondly, the committee, having asserted that the company's leadership was hapless, now succeeded in positioning them as unethical by highlighting that G4S would still seek to collect a huge management fee for a service which had not been properly managed. This ensured a continuation of the story long after the inquiry session had ended.

Lastly, the chair had got Buckles to accept that his job as CEO was now on the line, and that he should consider his own future. Unfortunately, Buckles gives the impression that he is indeed going to consider his own future, rather than providing any type of rebuttal which could have emphasised his otherwise impressive performance delivering record growth in the business worldwide. It would not have convinced the committee necessarily, but, in the absence of any evidence to the contrary, very few viewers would now see Buckles as anything other than a figure of ridicule.

Ultimately, G4S's reputation never fully recovered, even though they continue to provide many outsourced public services. When Buckles and Horseman-Sewell both eventually resigned, the committee got its scalps.

ANDY HAYMAN, FORMER MET POLICE ASSISTANT COMMISSIONER, HOME AFFAIRS COMMITTEE (JULY 2011)

BACKGROUND

Hayman was in charge of the initial inquiry into allegations of phone hacking by the *News of the World*, then the most popular newspaper in the UK. He took the decision at the time not to reopen the investigation when new evidence had apparently come to light.

In April 2010 it was reported by *The Guardian* that he subsequently 'left the police to work for News International [the owner of the *News of the World*] as a columnist'.[65] Allegations were therefore made that he was in cahoots with the very media organisation he was supposed to be investigating.

WHAT HAPPENED?

Hayman completely and totally misunderstood how a select committee works, especially one fronted by a chair, Keith Vaz, who had the ability to twist the knife and enjoy doing it. His evidence was far from convincing, but all that anyone who watched the session will remember was Hayman's extraordinary outburst of anger towards Conservative MP Lorraine Fullbrook and her Liberal Democrat colleague Dr Julian Huppert. Although the transcript below is highly entertaining, I would advise that this particular encounter is also watched online.[66]

KEY EXCHANGE

By this point in the committee session, Hayman had already

provided a series of unintentional moments of comedy. He had been pushed and probed on a number of allegations about his unethical behaviour while a senior member of the police, but the committee had not yet landed the killer blow. That all changed when the topic of illegal payments was raised.[67]

Lorraine Fullbrook: Mr Hayman, while a police officer did you receive payment from any news organisation?

Andy Hayman: Good God, absolutely not. I cannot believe you suggested that.

Julian Huppert: Lots of people did.

Andy Hayman: Hang on, I am not letting you get away with that. Absolutely no way. I can say to you—

Chair: Mr Hayman. Order.

Andy Hayman: No, come on, chairman, that is not fair.

Chair: Order, order.

Andy Hayman: That is not fair.

Chair: Mrs Fullbrook is not getting away with anything.

Andy Hayman: No, no, the additional comment.

Chair: It is the same question she had put to all witnesses.

Andy Hayman: Could Mr Huppert repeat his additional comment?

Julian Huppert: Other people have.

Andy Hayman: Yes, but hang on—

Chair: Mr Hayman. Order, Mr Hayman. Order.

Julian Huppert: There has been evidence in public that a number of police officers did.

Andy Hayman: But that is a real attack on my integrity. I am not having it.

Chair: Order, order. Members of this committee are allowed to ask any questions they wish. It is a fair question to put, because it is in the public domain at the moment about other police officers. She has put her question, you have given an answer. The answer is an unequivocal no.

Andy Hayman: Absolutely.

CONCLUSION

There are many terrible mistakes which select committee witnesses can make, but displays of anger towards MPs is just about the worst. The hearing, which would otherwise have been largely forgotten in the general noise at the time around phone hacking, suddenly became memorable because Hayman lost his temper. It gave permission for the media covering the event to go in with maximum vengeance.

In a sketch piece in the *Daily Telegraph*, Matthew Norman reported: 'At this unusually sombre moment in national life, Mr Hayman reduced that committee to astonished mirth. Its members were hardly in chuckle mode when he took his seat. Yet his performance, mingling breathtaking glibness with hilarious mock outrage, pierced the solemnity like a stiletto blade tipped with nitrous oxide.'[68]

In *The Guardian*, Simon Hoggart's analysis followed a similar thread: 'I've seen a few incredulous MPs in my time, but nothing like this. Through most of Mr Hayman's evidence they were either rolling with laughter, or favouring him with a cold, sardonic glare. Or both.'[69]

Needless to say, the final report from the committee was suitably damning and critical of Mr Hayman, and his comical appearance had again helped to position Keith Vaz as one of the toughest select committee chairs in Parliament.[70]

GREG CLARKE, THE FOOTBALL ASSOCIATION CHAIR, DIGITAL, CULTURE, MEDIA AND SPORT COMMITTEE (20 OCTOBER 2017)

BACKGROUND

Eniola Aluko was a leading footballer in the England women's national team. Her then manager Mark Sampson, once described as an 'English icon', is alleged to have made a racist joke to her about her family visiting from Nigeria and the spread of the Ebola virus. Sampson vehemently denied making racial remarks.

When the complaint was sent by the Professional Footballers' Association (PFA) to Greg Clarke, chair of the FA, he replied, 'I've no idea why you are sending me this. Perhaps you could enlighten me?' At best it was flippant and insensitive, but at worst it demonstrated that an organisation which purported to take racism seriously was doing no such thing.

The PFA had written to him to allege that the FA's former technical director, Dan Ashworth, and director of human resources, Rachel Brace, had overseen a sham inquiry to clear Mark Sampson of the allegation that he had also asked Drew Spence, a mixed-raced player, how many times she had been arrested. Clarke was facing questions about whether his appearance in front of the DCMS Committee should indicate his resignation.

WHAT HAPPENED?

In response to the story, the DCMS Committee explored how the FA conducted and managed internal investigations and complaints. The committee also considered the culture of the FA in relation to its governance structures and whether the attitudes of senior officials made it simple for aggrieved players to report instances of abuse.[71]

The committee took evidence from England women's stars Eniola Aluko and Lianne Sanderson and from FA representatives fronted by chair Greg Clarke and his CEO Martin Glenn.

KEY EXCHANGES

This session was a classic example of a senior representative going in to a select committee hearing hoping to extinguish fires, but ultimately creating entirely new ones through their blundering approach.

The Labour MP Jo Stevens is probing the relationship between the FA and the PFA. She is asking some very gentle questions to ascertain how tense the relationship between the two organisations may be.[72]

Jo Stevens: Will you be talking to the PFA?
Greg Clarke: I will be talking to the PFA, but let me be frank about my feeling for the PFA, and I would like to be very frank. I am pro-union, I am not anti-union. I

have worked with many unions over the years. Health and safety, protecting terms and conditions – I am not anti-union.

Jo Stevens: Are you a member of the union?

Greg Clarke: I have been a member of a union. No, I am not a member because there is no union for the likes of me. But I am pro-union. I put that on the card just so you know where I am coming from. When you look at the performance of the PFA, they have some really good executives and foot soldiers. I have fought with them, I have fought alongside them. When I say I have fought alongside them, we got the Rooney ruling in the Football League in cooperation with Kick It Out and the PFA, all trying to redress the outrageous lack of black managers in our game, which is absolutely appalling. So I have worked with them, I have worked against them. I have a fundamental problem with their governance at the top. Let me tell you why I have a fundamental problem.

Chair: We are here to talk about the governance of the FA not the PFA. We will do that another day. If we have time at the end I am happy to give you a chance to—

Greg Clarke: May I just have 30 seconds, just 30 seconds, and it will illustrate my point? I met a number of safeguarding survivors and it is a really important issue to me, some of them in formal meetings, some of them in informal meetings. I met a survivor who wept in the meeting in front of two FA witnesses, supportive people from safeguarding. He cried like a baby, a decent, honest person, because of what he had been through. I said, 'Is there anything you can do to help me?' He said, 'What can I do? The PFA will not pay for my counselling anymore.' The PFA spends millions of pounds a year on the CEO salary and the CEO pension fund and they are walking away from alcoholics, they are walking away from addicted gamblers and they are walking away from people like him. I will never look up to their governance but I respect their people.

•   •   •

Later, another Labour MP, Julie Elliott, is seeking to extract from Greg Clarke an acceptance that black players in the England women's team have been let down by the FA. It initially appears to be going well...

Julie Elliott: Do you think that you have a duty of care to the players of all of the England teams?

Greg Clarke: I do, yes.

Julie Elliott: If you do, you said your overwhelming duty of care was to victims.

Greg Clarke: Yes.

Julie Elliott: Clearly Eniola Aluko has been a victim.

Greg Clarke: Agreed.

Julie Elliott: Yet do you think your organisation fulfilled your duty of care to her?

Greg Clarke: No. The reason – one of the reasons I made such a point about governance – is it is really important in a governance role not to jump to conclusions. If I had have jumped to a conclusion halfway through this process and said, 'There is no problem here. Nothing has been found,' or whatever, you have to look in the end at what is established. What is established, putting aside all the fluff about institutional racism, no institutional bullying—

Chair: Do you call that fluff?

Greg Clarke: I am not trying to hide behind it.

Chair: You called it fluff. I do not think fluff is the word I would use to describe it.

Greg Clarke: The reason I say that is because Katharine Newton said there was no evidence of it. I could hide behind that. That is why I used that phrase.

Julie Elliott: But the fact that you describe that as fluff I think speaks volumes about the organisation.

Greg Clarke: No, no, please do not take it out of context.

Julie Elliott: Mr Clarke, you have said it. You have said it in evidence to a committee of the House of Commons. It speaks volumes. Language matters in any of these cases and you have just said fluff.

CONCLUSION

The media coverage of this hearing juxtaposed two things. On the one hand, there was the dignified evidence given by Aluko, who was understandably given a gentle set of questions by the chair and allowed to give a devastating insight into her experiences when subjected to prejudice. On the other hand, there was a middle-aged white man with a booming voice who lost his cool with the committee and revealed that, despite the spin, he did not really seem to believe that his organisation had done anything wrong.

What is most extraordinary about these two exchanges is that they were gifts given to the committee by Greg Clarke, which did not even require any particular skill in the questioning. He actually interrupts Damian Collins who was unknowingly about to help him by trying to move onto the next question. Instead, he demands another thirty seconds of time to launch a bizarre attack on the union that had been attempting to raise concerns about racist abuse.

However, the real crime was the subsequent reference to claims of institutional racism as 'fluff'. As you have seen, the committee immediately seized upon this incredible error and it ensured that whatever else the FA said in the remainder of the session, it could not win.

SIR PHILIP GREEN, ARCADIA GROUP CHAIR, WORK AND PENSIONS AND BUSINESS COMMITTEES (15 JUNE 2016)

BACKGROUND

Sir Philip Green is a British billionaire businessman and the chair of Arcadia Group, a retail company that includes Topshop, Topman, Wallis, Evans, Burton, Miss Selfridge, Dorothy Perkins and Outfit. The now defunct retailer BHS was once part of that same group.

Green bought BHS for £200 million in 2000, but the firm

performed poorly so he sold it for just £1 in 2015. By April 2016, BHS had debts of £1.3 billion, including a pensions deficit of £571 million.[73] Despite this, Green and his family collected £586 million in dividends, rental payments and interest on loans during their fifteen-year ownership of the retailer.

The Work and Pensions and Business select committees joined forces to summon Green to appear for a solo session. The combative businessman initially put up a fight, and took the remarkable step of writing to Frank Field to say that his participation in the hearing would only obstruct a resolution to the pensions issue: 'I am not prepared to participate in a process which has not even the pretence of fairness and objectivity and which has as its primary objective the destruction of my reputation, and I therefore require you to resign immediately from this inquiry.'[74] Unsurprisingly, this was rejected by Field, and only served to ramp up the tension when the hearing eventually took place.

WHAT HAPPENED?

Green faced one of the most gruelling select committee hearings in parliamentary history. Putting to one side his unpleasant characteristics, his nearly six-hour evidence session would have toppled almost any human being. He was pummelled by a group of MPs with literally no sympathy or willingness to believe a single word he was saying.

It was clear that Green knew that he could not win, although no one expected him to play to the theatre of the moment to quite the extent he did.

KEY EXCHANGES

There is a conspiracy theory I heard from people that have previous experience of working with Philip Green that what was considered a car-crash committee appearance was, in fact, largely a result of careful planning. The issue of whether Green behaved unethically as owner of BHS required careful analysis of the way the company was run under his stewardship. However, what most people remember from this session are the crazy antics that Green deployed at staggered intervals. He pulled out a cheque book at one point (I mean, who actually carries a cheque book in their jacket nowadays?), as well as an old mobile phone. In some ways, it is better for him that we remember the hearing for his erratic behaviour, rather than him being nailed on the specifics. The parliamentarian he tangles with in this exchange is Conservative MP Richard Fuller.[75]

> Sir Philip Green: The people I bought it [BHS] from had lost interest or – I don't know – lost their way with the business. Actually, it is about forty years; fifteen was BHS, so I can keep up with you. Basically, I think all these things that I said earlier stemmed from the product side. I think the buying was poor; the sourcing was pretty poor; there wasn't really an owner-driver driving the business. I worked pretty long hours going through each of the areas of the whole business, department by department, to understand what was working and what wasn't working. I didn't know any of the people in the building; they were all new to me. I hadn't been

in the building before. I think I'd been in there once before acquisition, so I didn't know any of the staff, so you have to start to get to know the people.

Coming back to something Michelle said, when you buy businesses from public companies or you buy public companies, the people have to trust you. Therefore when you get into these businesses, as a starting point you've got to get to know all of the people, because you've got to work with them.

I think we've got a pretty good track record as a company. In our existing business, the average stay in our head office is 11 or 12 years.

Sir, do you mind not looking at me like that all the time? It's really disturbing. [Interruption.] Sorry? You just want to stare at me? It's just uncomfortable, that's all.

Richard Fuller: I wasn't quite just staring at you, but I don't wish to make you uncomfortable.

Sir Philip Green: Sorry?

Richard Fuller: I don't wish to make you uncomfortable.

Sir Philip Green: No, but I'm just saying. It isn't somebody else; it's just uncomfortable, sort of staring at me.

• • •

The erratic behaviour continues, and as the session progresses he becomes even more combative with committee members, in this case two Conservative MPs, Jeremy Quin and Richard Fuller. Once again, the distraction allows Green to continue to run down the clock.

Jeremy Quin: I half agree with you; that was—

Sir Philip Green: You don't have to half agree; those are the facts.

Jeremy Quin: In the framework agreement, which I have got here, it was £6.5 million in cash and there was a lending agreement.

Sir Philip Green: Sorry?

Jeremy Quin: There was a loan of £3.5 million in addition to the £6.5 million cash—

Richard Fuller: Sorry, Jeremy. I am musing on a point that Iain Wright made. You have complained about Mr Quin putting his glasses on or not.

Sir Philip Green: Oh, I didn't complain; I was having a joke with him. Lighten up.

Richard Fuller: You have complained about me staring at you, and you have complained about the way in which questions are put to you. I just wonder, is that your usual pattern of behaviour, particularly with your directors?

Sir Philip Green: Shall we carry on?

Chair: You don't want to answer Mr Fuller?

Sir Philip Green: I am choosing to carry on with your colleague over here.

Chair: That is a very significant answer.

Sir Philip Green: What's that?

Chair: That you chose not to answer.

Sir Philip Green: No, I chose to ignore it. That's different.

Chair: I'm not so sure.

Sir Philip Green: That's another opinion.

Chair: Let's move on.

• • •

The session finishes with a flourish, as Green goes for a full apology from the chair, a demand which of course is rejected, but still acts as a distraction as it manages to disrupt the flow of the chair's concluding comments.

Chair: [Why did you not] Stop the deal?

Sir Philip Green: Which one?

Chair: The deal to buy BHS.

Sir Philip Green: Which deal?

Chair: Sports Direct's deal to buy BHS.

Sir Philip Green: There were two different times. One before, one after.

Chair: That's true.

Sir Philip Green: The one after?

Chair: Tell me which one – anything.

Sir Philip Green: Zero. Sir, I have offered to put money in. Look, let me just ask a sensible question to your whole committee. Basically, we have spent five or six hours. On what possible basis would I want to stop somebody buying it if they would rescue it? Why?

Chair: Ego.

Sir Philip Green: Oh, please – come on. That's an insult.

Chair: No, it's not.

Sir Philip Green: That's really rude.

Chair: No, it's a case of—

Sir Philip Green: I find that really rude.

Chair: I apologise; I don't mean to be rude, but in terms
of human nature—

Sir Philip Green: I think we got to hear—

Chair: You could not make a success of it—

Sir Philip Green: Excuse me—

Chair: You could not make a success of it and you did not
want another retail billionaire to do the same.

Sir Philip Green: I'm glad the meeting's ending. That's
disgusting, and it's a sad way to end.

Chair: We haven't finished yet, Sir Philip, if that's okay. We
have a number of things—

Sir Philip Green: I think that's out of order, and I think
you should apologise.

CONCLUSION

The Philip Green hearing is one of the key examples of the
strengths and weaknesses of select committees.

The combination of two strong committee chairs working
together for a common purpose ensured this session received
maximum coverage and reinforced the validity of its investigation. It also ensured that they could overcome Green's
attempts to wriggle out of answering for his actions when
owner of BHS, which was so important given the number of
pensioners who stood to suffer as a result. The fact they could
get him to give evidence suggests that a chair's dogged determination remains a vital function of the role. They also held
him for questioning beyond anyone's expectations, seemingly
adding minutes to the clock like a strict football referee every
time Green created his next piece of theatre.

On the downside, it is difficult to see what the committee got from Green after nearly six hours of interrogation. Yes, they got bucket-loads of coverage for those key moments around Green's accusations of 'staring', or his pulling out of props, but there was very little hard evidence to emerge from the session which could bring justice for the BHS pensioners and employees made redundant. It is not a view shared by all, but I think Green left that committee room with a vestige of a smile.

ARRON BANKS AND ANDY WIGMORE, LEAVE.EU, DIGITAL, CULTURE, MEDIA AND SPORT COMMITTEE (12 JUNE 2018)

BACKGROUND

The Digital, Culture, Media and Sport Committee hauled in Arron Banks and Andy Wigmore for a hearing about the relationship between their EU referendum campaign organisation Leave.EU and the controversial data firm Cambridge Analytica, as well as the use of data by Leave.EU and other bodies, such as Eldon Insurance and its brand, GoSkippy. This was part of the committee's inquiry into fake news.

It is worth noting that the committee comprised a predominantly Remain-leaning group.

The two men had played a card similar to Philip Green, seeking to avoid giving evidence on the basis of supposed committee bias. Banks announced in a letter published on Twitter: 'It is perfectly clear that the committee, which comprises only of remain supporting MPs, is conducting a co-ordinated "Witch

Hunt" of Leave groups involving the Electoral Commission & the ICO. You have called no witnesses from the Remain campaign or associated groups.' However, the committee got its way and both men appeared a few days later.

WHAT HAPPENED?

The two witnesses showed utter disdain for the select committee process, from the first invitation to the moment they walked out in a show of defiance. Unlike CEOs who represent mainstream companies and organisations, the figures from Leave.EU have long enjoyed playing up to their reputations, as the self-dubbed 'bad boys of Brexit'. There is very little reputational damage that they can sustain, given that people will have already largely made up their minds as to whether they are heroes or villains.

The entire session saw the pair play with the committee, being outrageous, confrontational and disrespectful, ending with a (probably) premeditated decision to walk out and therefore have the final word.

KEY EXCHANGES

Wigmore starts proceedings by cleverly pre-empting the accusations of collusion with powerful Russians which he knew were coming his way, instead proactively making similar allegations towards the chair. The reference to hospitality is pretty tenuous – Damian Collins was given tickets to watch a football team that is owned by a rich Russian – but it does immediately warn the committee that Wigmore and Banks do not intend to take their punishment quietly.[76]

Andy Wigmore: Mr chairman, in light of the fact that –
according to Guido – you had some hospitality from
Mr Putin's number one man in the United Kingdom,
do you not think you are a bit conflicted, quizzing us
about this today? I want to make a suggestion: perhaps
you might want to recuse yourself and let one of the
other people take over as chairman, so resign so you
can ask us questions independently.

Chair: It is a nice try, Mr Wigmore; you may have better
intel than me. I did not know that Roman Abramovich
was Putin's number one man in London, but you may
know more than I do. All I can say is that I got invited
to the football. I did not meet the owner and I was not
offered Stalin's vodka. I am not as good at pushing their
buttons as you are.

• • •

The Labour MP Christian Matheson begins to introduce the
concept of 'fake news' into the discussion but the witnesses
again hit back with venom, by adopting the populist view
that it is politicians who lie and cheat, thus attempting to
then undermine the further questions they will receive.

Christian Matheson: In the context of this inquiry, does that
include perhaps using fake news to shake people up?

Andy Wigmore: What is fake news? With great respect,
every politician uses the best-placed position of a situation to try to create the best environment for someone

to write about it. If that is fake news, then that is what we did. Fake news can come in many forms, if you want to examine it like that.

Arron Banks: I would say, Chris, that Parliament itself is the biggest source of fake news in the entire country.

Christian Matheson: I hope I could disagree with you on that one.

Arron Banks: Straight after this meeting you will be at lunch with a journalist from *The Guardian* quaffing a glass of Chablis and spinning it the way you want to spin it.

. . .

When the Conservative MP Rebecca Pow tries to suggest that Banks has an undue influence on politics, he uses self-deprecation to dispute the claim.

Rebecca Pow: It was just a general observation that all these different companies and names and tortuous, complicated arrangements that people now seem to be trying to unravel, journalists or whoever, suggest that you do have something to hide in all of this that might somehow have some connection to influencing politics across the world.

Arron Banks: I like to think I am an evil genius with a white cat that controls the whole of western democracy, but clearly that is nonsense.

. . .

Under a final barrage of difficult questioning from Labour's Ian Lucas, Banks creates the key moment everyone remembers from the session: his decision to walk out of the committee hearing to attend a lunch. However, even this was after Banks asks whether the same MP had committed drunken sexual harassment on a woman in a parliamentary bar (he had not). The three following exchanges do not run directly in sequence, but demonstrate how quickly the session descended into often childish acrimony.

> Ian C. Lucas: Mr Banks, before July 2011, was Southern Rock investigated by the Gibraltar Finance Services Committee?
>
> Arron Banks: No, I am now not going to answer any more questions on the insurance business. I have covered it with – is it Rebecca? You can read what you like from that, but I have given the explanation to a pretty full list of questions.
>
> Ian C. Lucas: I just want to know, is that the case? Why don't you answer the question?
>
> Arron Banks: I have given you an answer.
>
> Ian C. Lucas: You have not given me an answer. You are avoiding.
>
> Arron Banks: I have said, I have answered the question.
>
> Ian C. Lucas: You are not answering a straight question.
>
> Arron Banks: I have answered the questions on my financial affairs. I am not going to answer any more questions.
>
> Ian C. Lucas: Are you going to answer any questions about your financial affairs?

Arron Banks: I just have, in full.

Ian C. Lucas: I am asking you another question about your financial affairs.

Arron Banks: Well, you can ask away. I am not going to answer any more questions on that.

Ian C. Lucas: I just want to be clear, so you are—

Andy Wigmore: What relevance has this to do with fake news?

Ian C. Lucas: I am speaking to Mr Banks.

Andy Wigmore: I don't care. I am speaking as well. What relevance has this to do with the referendum and fake news? What relevance has it got to do with it?

• • •

Arron Banks: Are you the MP that got drunk in the House of Commons and harassed a woman and got drunk on a karaoke evening?

Ian C. Lucas: No.

Arron Banks: Good, but one of the committee is. I just don't know who. What do you want me to do? Do we want to sit here and throw bread rolls at each other?

Ian C. Lucas: Mr Banks, I think this is a serious issue.

Arron Banks: Why?

• • •

Andy Wigmore: Chairman, you said 20 minutes and I genuinely do have another appointment that I do not want to be late for.

Chair: Is it just one or two questions, Ian?

Arron Banks: I am sorry, I really have to insist. I was told a certain time and we have a luncheon appointment that we do not want to be late for.

Andy Wigmore: You can join us if you want, we will be in the—

Chair: Could you just give us five minutes?

Arron Banks: No, you said when you left 20 minutes and now we have run way past 20 minutes, so I am sorry but I am afraid that it is time to go. We have been as open as we could be with the issues you have raised.

Chair: I appreciate the time, but I would be grateful if you could just give us five minutes so Mr Lucas can finish his question.

Arron Banks: The word is no. When you went out you said 20 minutes, and I think we have run past 20 minutes and I am sorry but there it is.

Chair: Mr Lucas said he does not wish to pursue his question, so we will leave it there.

CONCLUSION

Even more so than Philip Green, here were two witnesses determined to distract, deflect and appear before a select committee on their own terms. Both Banks and Wigmore knew that there was no one there to persuade and potentially win over. They were fully aware that the final report of the committee would slam them for the role they played in the EU referendum and how they used data during the campaign, and accuse them of inappropriate links with Russia.

In the words of Collins himself:

The unelected Banks is now displaying a consistent pattern of behaviour where he constantly seeks to abuse and
intimidate politicians and journalists – and he is not the
only one. This is partly just attention seeking, but it also
has a more sinister edge. Unchecked, this is the kind of
behaviour that allows the virus of fascism to seep into
democracy.[77]

Select committees work best when a private sector witness
has something to lose. If they represent a regulated company
with exposure to the competition authorities, or are battling
for a good price review process, a bad select committee
hearing could have huge financial consequences. Similarly,
if the executive represents a listed company and admits to
massive failings in the organisation, as in the case of G4S
and the 2012 Olympics, shareholders can demonstrate their
significant displeasure by forcing them out. None of this applied to Banks and Wigmore.

Narrowing down my choice of memorable select committee hearings was not easy, as there have been many moments
of high drama. Of course, these are not representative of most
hearings, hundreds of which pass by each year without attracting major comment. However, it is notable that the clear majority of examples I could have included have occurred since
the election of independent chairs in 2010. With the continued interest from committees in grilling corporate leaders, we
are likely to see further theatrics in the coming years.

INTERNATIONAL COMPARISONS

Before we look at some of the policy ideas provided by a range of informed select committee watchers and participants whom I interviewed, I have also examined how some other notable Parliaments around the world organise their own committee systems.

INFLUENCE ON POLICY

Although our select committees are distinctive, they are not unusual – most large Parliaments have committees to help make policy and law. However, where international committees are responsible for directly shaping legislation, they become much more deeply embedded in the parliamentary process and the work of government departments. This contrasts with their UK equivalents, which provide only an oversight.

In the United States, there is a culture of deference towards the stronger committees that possess a legislative capacity and have powers of veto over what pieces of legislation go forward to the House. Senator Sam Ervin, who chaired the Watergate Committee that helped to unseat President Richard Nixon, said congressional investigations 'can be the catalyst that spurs Congress and the public to support vital reforms in our nation's laws'.[78]

However, they are now considered less independent of the policy agendas of their party leaders than they used to be and more restricted in terms of developing their own legislative initiatives. In the case of Watergate, it was rival parties working together for a common cause which ultimately ensured that it defeated the President. It is difficult to imagine that happening in the more partisan politics of today.

In Europe, Germany has the most influential and politically balanced legislative committee structure. It is closely integrated into the consensual style of German politics, and therefore differs from the partisan politics of the House of Commons. As a result, committee reports in Germany are commonly accepted in their entirety by government and in Parliament.

POWERS TO COMPEL WITNESSES

A number of countries have tougher powers at their disposal than the UK Parliament.

In France, for example, the standing committees have the right to summon any person of their choice, and failure to reply is punishable by a £7,500 fine.[79]

Although few other countries have such a clear financial penalty for resistant witnesses, they tend to have much more clearly defined powers. The committees in the United States are much tougher on compelling witnesses to attend: 'Congressional contempt authority may take one of three forms: inherent, civil, or criminal. Failure to adhere to committee rules during an investigation may thus have severe legal consequences.'[80]

Similarly, in Australia, each House is able to punish offences which interfere with the work of a committee. As the official guidance says, somewhat menacingly, 'If a person refuses to attend, or a witness refuses to answer a question, lies or misleads a committee, they may be punished by reprimand, fine or imprisonment.'[81]

German committees are more focused on ensuring access to elected decision-makers, and have the power to demand the attendance of a member of the federal government at any meeting, as well as the right to access files and documents.

However, in New Zealand, committees lost their power to summon witnesses in 1999, and now have an approach which is much closer to the UK's own, hoping the reputational risk is too great to say no.[82] As the Parliament itself describes, 'The new procedures have been developed to ensure due deliberation is built into the exercise of these powers, which are used rarely.'[83] However, they can approach the Speaker to issue a summons or may do so themselves with the leave of the House.

MEMBERSHIP

In many major legislatures, serving on a parliamentary committee is the norm rather than an exception. In Germany, for example, every MP serves on a committee, and it could be argued that this helps to prevent vetoes or other manipulation by party managers and whips. As per the system in the UK, the committee chairs are also appointed in line with the balance of the parliamentary groups in the Bundestag as a whole, but unlike the UK, German committees have a formal position of deputy chair substitutes to deputise for members in their absence.

In the US Congress, service on committees has long been a significant and respected career choice, although committee chairs receive only the same salary as other members, albeit with larger allowances for office costs.

However, the increased independence of UK chairs (as of their election by all members of the House since 2010) has distinguished us from many other countries, where the influence of the main political parties on committees is considered greater.

RESOURCES

The committees of the US Congress are very powerful bodies which command huge staffs and substantial resources, but European legislative committees generally share the UK's problem of stretched time and money. This is because most European parliamentary committees combine their responsibilities for reviewing, shaping and in some cases initiating legislation, as well as UK-style duties such as shadowing the policy-making of government departments.

However, some countries have other resources at their disposal. For example, official funding for committees in Germany is modest, but political parties and party-related education and research foundations receive some state funding. Committee members are therefore well supported from a research perspective.

CONCLUSION

What my research into international committees shows is that the UK has had a huge influence on the rest of the world (as has generally been the case with our parliamentary system) and still stands out as an example of more rigorous examination of the decisions which impact on our everyday lives. However, a number of countries have taken the decision to assert their authority in a much more significant way, especially in their powers to compel witnesses to attend. Other countries have committees which make a much more meaningful impression on public policy without the histrionics we sometimes see closer to home. In some cases, they are also better resourced.

Although we are not majorly out of step with the rest of the world, there is always room for improvement and our ambition for the UK committee system should be as high as possible. With this in mind, Part 2 explores some potential policy ideas which could effect that change.

PART 2

HOW TO IMPROVE A SELECT COMMITTEE

'The minute somebody joins a committee … they immediately suffer from committee brain. They become wildly over-enthusiastic, over-optimistic, over-pessimistic. Committees turn people into idiots and politics is a committee.'

P. J. O'ROURKE
POLITICAL SATIRIST

INTRODUCTION

What does the future hold for departmental select committees as we approach their 40th anniversary, and the 10th anniversary of the publication of the Wright Report? It is a question which has been on my mind since I began interviewing committee chairs for this book. I did not initially envisage creating a section which explored the future of select committees and some of the policy options available to improve them. However, as I interviewed a range of informed thinkers and practitioners – senior chairs, previous witnesses, journalists and think-tank specialists – it became abundantly clear to me that this milestone presents a crucial opportunity on which to reflect on whether the system is working as it should. If we conclude it is not, then how do we best fix it?

The biggest challenge – and opportunity – is how to minimise the knee-jerk responses from the committees and, instead, get them to focus on longer-term policy issues. We do need select committees to continue to hold powerful elected and non-elected people to account, but to do so in a manner which steers away from the populist cynicism that condemns those in positions of power as guilty unless proven innocent. To deploy the same dramatic language often used by committees themselves, they are feasting upon corporate woes, partly because it is an irresistible opportunity for profile-raising. But what if something more substantive could replace this tendency to showboat?

As Conservative MP (and former member of Margaret Hodge's renowned Public Accounts Committee) Steve Barclay told *The Spectator* in 2013:

> Critics are right to challenge the current performance of select committees; but they are wrong in the lazy assertion that all MPs want from these sessions is to grandstand. The incentive for many MPs is to do the job they were elected to do: holding bodies to account on behalf of their constituents. Many of us prefer to use the microscope to the blunderbuss. Parliament needs to update its tools.[84]

Part of the updating of these 'tools' is to invest in committees (both in terms of money and training) to enable them to return to their original function of shadowing the work of the relevant department(s) and measuring the long-term impacts of government policy, and to rely less on the ritual humiliation of corporates and public officials. As the excellent Institute for Government stated in its latest review of Parliament's effectiveness, 'Whether select committees continue to provide an attractive option for experienced members will depend on the frequency with which they undertake high profile work or work which is seen to have real impact on government.'[85]

As we have already explored, the year 2010 was unquestionably a watershed moment for select committees, as it is when chairs became elected by cross-party MPs rather than by the grace and favour of party managers. It also coincided with a change of government and the beginning of austerity, as the UK fumbled around for economic responses to the credit crunch created by the global financial crisis.

The combination of emboldened select committees and the demonisation of business has created a perfect storm. We now have the bankers, the alleged tax dodgers, the auditors and the maverick business leaders such as Mike Ashley and Philip Green to beat up. We have had the collapse of high street companies, new threats posed to cybersecurity, the foreign policy challenges of Russia and the rise of ISIS. The world around us seems to be in the midst of the most intense change, with the relentless rise of populism and the issues posed by technology, especially the automation of jobs.

Select committees now have a major opportunity to rise to these challenges, to scrutinise policy and, in doing so, improve it. We have seen, as the main political parties become more polarised and fundamentalist in their policy-making, a greater influx of talented people into the select committee system in recent years. These are people who, in the main, feel frustrated that their talents are not being fully utilised in a Cabinet or shadow Cabinet capacity. We should harness this talent to make sure our select committees are the best in the world, even if the overall quality of our politics seems to be on a downward trajectory.

The following policy ideas were not dreamt up by me on a whim. They were all suggested to me during my interviews with people who have strong understanding and knowledge of the select committee process, but from vastly different positions of self-interest. Some of these ideas will probably prove to be difficult to implement and possibly have unintended consequences, but that does not mean we should not at least open the debate. What I have attempted to do is to outline the thinking behind each idea and then assess the pros and cons. Hopefully this will spark some fresh thinking about how we can maximise the undoubted benefits of select committees and strengthen them as a crucial function of Parliament.

RESOURCES AND RULES

STRENGTHEN THE RULES
TO COMPEL WITNESSES

BACKGROUND

Despite tough talk for many years from a succession of select committee chairs, it is generally agreed that they no longer have any formal ability to compel witnesses to attend. There is still confusion over what documents select committees have access to, as demonstrated by the dispute between the Public Accounts Committee with the BBC over the names of senior executives who received payoffs.[86] Steve Barclay goes as far to suggest, 'Parliament appears afraid to use its historic powers for fear that it will be challenged in the European courts.'

Back in 1978, the House of Commons:

> resolved that its penal jurisdiction should be exercised a) as sparingly as possible and b) only when the House is satisfied that to exercise it is essential in order to provide reasonable protection for the House, its Members or its

officers, from … substantial interference with the performance of their respective functions.[87]

Since then, Parliament has agonised over whether it has needed to tool up its powers, but has yet to effectively take any direct action. In 2012, the Liaison Committee did conclude that while the current system was not broken, action should be taken to head off a potential crisis in the future, and therefore a 'do-nothing' strategy was not sufficient to meet the new challenges the committees face.

The best we currently have is the weighty language of a formal summons and, often more effective, the power of embarrassment for those who resist the overtures of a committee. Certainly in my experience with corporates, the threat of bad personal PR is usually enough to force their hand. However, as we saw in Part 1, this often does not seem to bother those without anything obvious to lose, especially if they have positioned themselves as anti-establishment rebels, such as key members of the Vote Leave campaign during the 2016 EU referendum. In the past, both Houses have had the power to imprison and, in the case of the Lords, to fine an individual who committed a 'contempt', such as refusing to appear before a committee or giving misleading evidence. However, the last occasion on which the Commons imprisoned anyone was when Queen Victoria was still on the throne.

Today, the consequences for committing a contempt are, in practice, limited to admonishment, and even that is not deployed very frequently. For example, in September 2016, following a nine-year investigation by the Committee of

Privileges, the Commons resolved to reprimand two employees of News International, Colin Myler and Tom Crone,
for deliberately misleading the Culture, Media and Sport
Committee about their knowledge of phone hacking. Subsequently, the House asked the Committee of Privileges to
undertake an inquiry into the matter of 'the exercise and
enforcement of the powers of the House in relation to select
committees and contempts'.[88] The committee launched a
new inquiry into the powers of select committees in March
2017, but its initial work was interrupted by the general election a few months later; this investigation is ongoing, with
little sign of a conclusion in the short-to-medium term.[89]

As the Institute for Government has outlined, in recent
years, instances of non-government witnesses contemplat-
ing refusing to give evidence to Commons committees have
become more frequent. Both Rupert and James Murdoch
(chair and chief executive of News International at the
time), Philip Green at BHS and the colourful Mike Ashley of
Sports Direct eventually gave in to media pressure to attend,
after a lengthy process. However, Irene Rosenfeld of Kraft
simply refused to budge when she judged the downsides of
appearing strongly outweighed the benefits. More recently,
both Mark Zuckerberg, CEO of Facebook, and Dominic
Cummings, former director of Vote Leave, chose to face
off the authority of the Digital, Culture, Media and Sport
Committee to call them as witnesses. Cummings is a UK
citizen, which means he should not have been able to refuse,
but if Zuckerberg were on UK soil, the summons should, in
theory, have applied to him too.

Beyond the summoning of witnesses, there is also a challenge for select committees to be equipped with key source material. For example, consultants PwC undertook a review of Universal Credit, which was not shared until the night before a Work and Pensions Committee hearing. Furthermore, the Public Accounts Committee had to pen a report on Universal Credit without access to a key external review by the person overseeing the project, which left the committee's report lacking key insights on the pivotal issue of IT implementation.[90] It is reasonable to suggest that select committees need access to both people and vital information in order to scrutinise effectively.

PROPOSED SOLUTION

What has become clear in the process of researching the powers of select committees is how unclear their powers actually are. What is undeniable is that the presumed powers of select committees are not set out or enforceable in a way that is consonant with the modern legal system.

Parliament is currently looking at whether it would be desirable to have clearer definitions and enforcement powers, which would probably involve some form of statute to enable the courts to act as the enforcer on Parliament's behalf. The alternative is to stick with the status quo, where the powers remain theoretically boundless, but limited in practice.

To afford the select committees the necessary standing, many argue that they need to formalise their powers to compel witnesses in a way which eliminates, once and for all, any doubt as to how Parliament is able to exert the will of the people. In the words of the Institute for Government, 'The scrutiny conducted by select committees would be strengthened if their right to use their powers to sanction people for refusing to attend or providing misleading testimony was reaffirmed in statute.'[91]

Bringing our select committees' powers more in line with those enjoyed by committees in the United States would be a very significant policy change. US congressional committees are significantly more powerful than their UK counterparts due to the power of subpoena, which means that witnesses and evidence can be requested to come before the committee, or face sanctions. Therefore, adopting a similar system in the UK would not be without precedent. For example, committees could be granted the power:

- to compel witnesses to attend or risk facing tangible legal sanctions;
- to compel an individual, organisation or government department to produce documents upon request; and
- to penalise an individual who can be proven to have misled a committee.

The format of these new powers would need to be determined by Parliament, but, in essence, select committee chairs would be given legally binding authority to summon specific witnesses present in the UK, with the threat of imprisonment for those who refuse and thereby show contempt of Parliament.

Helpfully, the Clerk of the House (effectively the chief

executive of Parliament) has produced an illustrative draft clause demonstrating how the House could use the courts to enforce orders to attend a select committee:

Failure to attend Commons Select Committee

(1) This section applies if the Speaker of the House of Commons certifies that an individual–

    (a) was summoned by a Select Committee of the House of Commons to attend the Committee to answer questions or to provide information or documents, and

    (b) has failed to attend, or to answer questions or to provide information or documents.

(2) The Speaker may certify in writing to the High Court that the individual has failed to comply with the summons.

(3) Where a failure to comply is certified under subsection (2), the court–

    (a) shall inquire into the matter, and

    (b) may make an order, or

    (c) may deal with the individual as if for a contempt of court.

(4) The court may act under subsection (3)(b) after hearing–

    (a) any witness who may be produced on behalf of the Committee,

    (b) any statement that may be offered on behalf of the individual, and

(c) any witness who may be produced on behalf of the individual.

(5) The court may consider the nature and purpose of the Committee's summons and proceedings for the purposes of determining what action (if any) to take under subsection (3)(b) (but not for any other purpose, and this section does not diminish or qualify any existing right or privilege of the House of Commons).[92]

I think this draft demonstrates that it is possible to provide a simple outline which strengthens Parliament's powers in a way which is likely to deter those tempted to defy the will of a select committee. After all, the best laws are those which prevent the offence from taking place at all.

PROS

Granting increased powers of summons would represent one of the most important moments in the history of the select committees, making clear that accountability to the electorate is a fundamental principle which everyone must understand and take seriously.

The idea that an arrogant individual or company could simply refuse to explain their actions is unacceptable; recently, some have even been emboldened by the success of certain witnesses' provocative 'come and get me' approach. If the committees are seen to lack muscle, then respect for their standing inevitably falls across a whole range of stakeholders, including the public. In the words of the Clerk of the House, 'the wider public would be likely to draw conclusions from any sustained refusal to co-operate with an inquiry'.[93]

By implementing genuine powers of summons, we would prevent the ridiculous scenes of witnesses refusing to appear, knowing that to do so under the new rules could lead to a criminal sanction. Despite some of the concerns that have been raised, the balance of opinion in the Commons seems to have shifted towards creating some form of statutory offence, such as contempt of Parliament, and now is the moment to help future-proof the system.

CONS

The select committees already have the ability to exert some of the powers outlined above, such as demanding witness attendance and access to documentation, and most of the time their informal influence is enough to secure the right outcome. To go beyond the current system, which would require passing legislation, for the sake of the handful of individuals who have refused to attend, is arguably an inefficient use of significant time and effort. Former Leader of the House David Lidington MP highlighted the informal consequences of not appearing:

Refusing to attend Select Committees as a witness … causes reputational damage for the perpetrator. Being designated as having committed a contempt of Parliament or having even been described as not a 'fit and proper' person to hold a particular office or exercise a particular function can cause reputational damage to the individual and can also cause commercial damage to the organisations they represent.[94]

The proposed changes would be difficult to implement due to our unique constitutional arrangement, which precludes the courts from becoming involved in matters of Parliament. This is something that Parliament has been assessing for many years, and about which has still not reached a conclusion. In 2016, the Institute for Government suggested: 'For all sorts of practical, legal and constitutional reasons, it is highly doubtful that the modern House would seriously consider this.'[95]

To put this into practice, imprisoning a UK citizen for not being willing to appear in front of a group of parliamentarians (who are potentially focused on humiliating them in front of live cameras) is surely unfair. In short, the select committees must respect the rights of witnesses and observe a form of due process which does not override their basic human rights.

Most key witnesses summoned, and insisted upon, by select committees do actually attend under the current system, so this measure may be seen as both disproportionate and ripe for exploitation. If select committee chairs do indeed delight in attracting publicity, they may be incredibly tempted to be the first to send a reluctant witness to prison.

INCREASE THE COMMITTEES' FINANCIAL RESOURCES

BACKGROUND

One of the biggest issues which emerged countless times in my interviews with committee chairs and officials was the insufficient financial resources available to fund their work. This lack of money can have dire consequences for the quality of the committees' output. Conversely, many witnesses before those same committees have the ability to spend significant sums of money to be trained professionally. Even ministers and senior officials have access to bespoke training from within the civil service. These private companies and ministries can throw money at the challenges they face. The committees often do not have that opportunity, and instead find themselves muddling along and doing the best that they can.

The Institute for Government has calculated, based on data from the 2016/17 session, that the average staffing costs of a Commons select committee are around £500,000 annually. Additionally, a select committee incurs approximately £26,000 of expenses per financial year, which includes the cost of special advisors, overseas visits and witnesses' expenses.

These figures look very reasonable when you put them in the context of Parliament's overall budget of £551 million per year, which itself is only roughly equivalent to administering a mid-sized government department.[96] Although the costs of running Parliament may seem like a significant sum of taxpayers' money, I would argue that it is surprisingly good value, and there is a strong case for providing it with more, as long as it can demonstrate the additional benefits. In return for this money, legislation is scrutinised and committees undertake vital inquiries into a range of relevant policy topics, but the whole operation requires Parliament to have the right people and resources to deliver.

Another indirect area in which committee resources are lacking is the funding for the offices of the MPs who chair them. While there is an additional salary boost for chairs, there is no increase in their budget for the running of their parliamentary office. If an MP devotes the time required to maximise the activities of his or her committee, then it adds a significant additional burden for their parliamentary staff, especially given the limited committee resources available.

PROPOSED SOLUTION

Select committees have been a hugely successful function of Parliament, despite being both under-resourced and over-worked. If we truly believe they do a vital job in holding the powerful and elected to account on our behalf, then one of the best uses of public money is to provide them with additional financial support. The level of increased funding for select committees may have to be part of a wider overall increase to the running of Parliament, and would therefore need to be carefully discussed and judged on deliverable improvements. But an initial assessment should be made of each public-facing select committee to ascertain their needs and how more money could be put to good use. The committees would produce a forward plan of 'aspirations', which would outline their topic areas for long-term inquiry.

A statement from each committee at the end of each parliamentary year would provide transparency about where the money was spent and the key achievements in that period.

Additionally, it would be highly beneficial to increase a chair's own office budget so that the MP is able to employ an advisor who focuses solely on the work of the committee. That advisor should also be given the authority to attend private committee meetings, so that they can act as a de facto committee advisor.

PROS

The select committee members I interviewed unanimously expressed the view that the committees would benefit significantly from increased funding. One said, 'I completely agree with this idea, as the role of select committees has expanded dramatically. It is important that committees have the resources necessary to carry out their important work.' Select committees receive too little money from the public purse in comparison to the importance of the function which they fulfil and this must be remedied.

This lack of financial backing means that many of the committees, as one other chair stated, 'make do and mend', having to cobble together what they can in order to function properly. The comparatively small budgets leave the committees at an immediate disadvantage, especially when you consider the financial muscle of those they question. Select committees perversely begin at a disadvantage when up against big multinational corporations, when it should surely be the other way round.

The lack of investment in committees is often linked to the poor-quality questioning we sometimes see. Committee chairs cannot get access to the right people to do the right research, achieve the right insights and therefore ask the right questions. This means many business executives and ministers get to avoid the hardest questions, and the public is none the wiser.

Extra money would mean that the committees could start securing additional talent and supercharge the process of holding people to account. The questions would be more insightful, the seriousness of the committees would increase and the overall process would elicit greater respect. Margaret Hodge did get extremely good senior advisors to help her during the sessions examining the tax affairs of multinationals, but she also got lucky in finding top people who were willing to give their time for free. Quality parliamentary scrutiny should not be a game of chance.

Increasing funding would also be an opportunity to balance some of the resource disparities between the committees. In any scenario, the big-name committees such as Treasury and Foreign Affairs will always attract good people, but what about less glamorous ones such as Housing, Communities and Local Government, or Public Administration and Constitutional Affairs? They still do very valuable work, but their ability to attract big talent in their respective fields is much diminished in comparison. I would begin with a review of each select committee for their current capabilities, the number of long-term and short-term inquiries which were undertaken during the past two parliamentary terms and their needs for the future. The result could be some form of what local authorities used to refer to as 'resource equalisation' (i.e. where a more consistent level of funding is agreed across multiple parties) or a bidding process based upon this review.

CONS

The public already considers the cost of politics to be too high and therefore providing additional taxpayer funds may not be popular at a time when austerity in public services continues to bite. It could also be argued that the current system delivers a good service for the public on its existing budget, and there is no direct evidence that increasing funds will increase quality.

If Parliament is going to struggle to secure additional public money, especially after approving £5.6 billion of building repairs to the Palace of Westminster, then spending extra millions on select committees may not be feasible. It would also have to ensure that any extra spending on external advisors is monitored carefully to guarantee that the taxpayer is getting value for their money, and that it is not being spent inappropriately.

RE-ESTABLISH REGIONAL SELECT COMMITTEES

BACKGROUND

As I mentioned in Part 1, when Gordon Brown became Prime Minister in the summer of 2007, he sought to pursue a renewed agenda of devolution, elements of which at the time were strongly resisted by the opposition Conservative Party. As part of that policy push, he appointed regional ministers for England and sought to make them accountable, a change which was reflected in the select committee system. The Labour government produced a Green Paper, grandly titled 'The Governance of Britain', and the idea eventually appeared in a report by the Select Committee on the Modernisation of the House of Commons, called 'Regional Accountability'.[97]

Pursuant to legislation laid down by the Labour government, select committees were appointed to examine the following English regions: East Midlands; East of England; north-east; north-west; south-east; south-west; West Midlands; and Yorkshire and the Humber.

The Communities and Local Government Committee agreed with the government that one means of achieving this scrutiny could be the establishment of regional select committees, the potential benefits of which include effective examination of the work of regional bodies and calling ministers to account. In oral evidence, the then chair of the committee, Dr Phyllis Starkey, gave her view that the purpose of parliamentary accountability would be 'to scrutinise a fairly limited number of regional bodies, such as, obviously, the RDAs, also strategic health authorities, learning and skills councils, maybe slightly more'.[98]

These committees were established in November 2008, with the London Regional Committee added later, in June 2009. Each regional committee would consist of no more than nine MPs, and they would remain members of that committee for the remainder of the parliamentary term. The purpose of the London committee was slightly different, as it was specifically charged with examining the government's relationship with the Greater London Authority. One member of the London committee was a then largely forgotten backbench left-winger named Jeremy Corbyn.

All nine committees ceased to exist upon the dissolution of Parliament in April 2010, and were never to be seen again upon the formation of the Conservative–Liberal Democrat coalition government.

PROPOSED SOLUTION

Select committees, just like other functions of Parliament, are disproportionately focused on people and issues in and around London. Yes, there has been a gradual increase in committee sessions taking place outside of London, but they often feel like token gestures for the sake of publicity.

Instead, special joint initiatives between committees would examine issues relevant to specific regions on a regular basis. They would be held at an easily accessible venue such as town halls in Birmingham, Manchester and Newcastle, and would be focused on a topic decided in consultation with the relevant regional authorities, mayors (where applicable) and other local bodies.

As with their short-lived predecessors in 2008–10, the regional select committees would meet significantly less frequently than departmental select committees, partly to answer the criticism that MPs do not have sufficient time for this additional responsibility.

Another idea could be to introduce set targets for the number of regional visits and hearings for select committees, so that each committee, for example, has to hold five evidence sessions in relevant regions during each parliamentary year.

PROS

People in the English regions are often reported to feel disconnected to what is happening in Westminster, reflected in some ways by the patterns of voting in the 2016 EU referendum (for instance, 58.8 per cent in the East Midlands chose to leave; 58 per cent in the north-east; and 57.7 per cent in Yorkshire and Humber).[99] Understanding the issues and concerns people in other regions face, therefore, is increasingly important to ensure area-specific problems are spotted as they arise.

The regional committees would be a small but meaningful way of showing that Westminster is listening to and coordinating with local governments. The membership would be composed of cross-party MPs who represent the region in question, and hopefully bring a greater degree of opponents working together for the common good (dependent on the party representation in any given area). It would also mean relevant ministers would be held to direct account in the areas in which a difficult policy decision was taken. For example, when the Secretary of State for Transport, Rt Hon. Chris Grayling MP, announced the ending of the electrification project for trains in the north-west, he would have had to appear in Liverpool or Manchester to explain why, as well as in Parliament itself.

The combination of select committees providing opportunities for inquiries and reports into regional policy and administration, together with opportunities for debate involving all MPs from the relevant area, would provide a major step forward in the scrutiny of regional policy.

Ministers responsible for policies which impact particular regions should be accountable to Parliament. Both they and the government's regional policy should therefore be subject to formal and consistent parliamentary scrutiny.

CONS

In reality, we have to ask whether there would be much interest in a regional select committee. The public is already turned off and weary of formal, mainstream politics and just adding a new layer of political representation to the mix is unlikely to suddenly reawaken interest in the activities in Westminster. The committees would do their best, they would huff and puff, but ultimately meaningful change would still be difficult to deliver.

There may be more effective ways to achieve a greater regional focus within Parliament without seeking to establish new committees, and select committees already have a means of ensuring that regional issues do come to light. For example, the Digital, Culture, Media and Sport Committee published a report in December 2016 on countries of culture, which assessed arts funding outside of London. Most of the departmental select committees hold visits and evidence sessions across the UK, and we should seek to encourage more of this, rather than setting up entirely new groups.

Deciding how to divide up regional committees could be challenging, as could their membership, if MPs simply use them as tools to increase their own chance of retaining their seats at the next general election. This was a problem identified the last time regional select committees were set up, and it led to significant problems related to the composition of the regional groups. This is exacerbated by the fact that many areas of England have solely one-party representation. The opposition could, for example, decide to use a regional select committee as a tool to embarrass the government on a topical issue, such as the use of food banks in the northwest. This would then cease to be about understanding policy effects in a reasoned way, and instead become yet another means by which select committees are used to garner publicity.

Furthermore, Parliament has so many committees, including those which do not just focus on external issues (e.g. the Committee of Privileges or the Backbench Business Committee) that simply finding enthused and willing members to join a new set of committees might be difficult. When you deduct the numbers of MPs who are on the government payroll, and those who have senior positions amongst the opposition, there are not huge numbers of people to fill all the various roles which parliamentary business creates.

MEMBERSHIP

PROVIDE PROFESSIONAL TRAINING FOR SELECT COMMITTEE MEMBERS

BACKGROUND

Dr Marc Geddes of the University of Edinburgh has researched attitudes to select committee membership and concluded that MPs use this work as a way to gain expertise in different policy areas or build on previous professional experience. Furthermore, committee service enhances professional skills, such as learning different questioning techniques, and provides structure to parliamentary work. This seems especially important to help socialise newly elected MPs.[100]

Some MPs are fortunate to come to Parliament with these skills. One chair said they had benefited from a career in the law: 'Fortunately I did have a previous career which prepared me in how to ask questions, and that has been invaluable and has made me more effective.'

However, one former MP who served on several select committees during his time in Parliament told me that arriving with this expertise is unusual, and the commitment of the various chairs and principal committee clerks to the training of members differs vastly. This produces committees of a very disjointed range of quality. He also told me that most MPs do not commit to anything more than a box-ticking approach to training once they join a select committee, even for the first time. There is often a starters' briefing pack provided, but ultimately each MP makes it up as they go along until they develop enough experience to feel comfortable in their new role. This is surely not good enough, given how important select committees are to challenging policies, people and institutions.

The briefings provided to MPs, the preparation they undertake and the skill with which they intervene in evidence sessions are crucial to committee effectiveness. We need them ready from the get-go. As one current chair told me: 'We need specialist knowledge to do our jobs properly and we greatly benefit from outside expertise. We often need to know what the answer to a question should be – not just the clever questions to ask.'

PROPOSED SOLUTION

A much more rigorous and formalised training process is required to upskill our members of Parliament, in order to improve the quality of questioning on select committees. This could be in the form of a compulsory training programme, and newly elected committee members would be allowed to proceed only once they had completed the training modules.

MPs seeking to become a member of a parliamentary select committee would initially be offered the opportunity for an in-depth briefing as to the role and expectations of what the position entails. This would allow them the opportunity to reflect on whether they wish to commit that level of time and energy to it. They would be given very clear guidance on the expectations in relation to attendance levels, attention to detail and the overall purpose of the role. Once selected, the training would encompass how to conduct evidence sessions, the process of drafting reports and a module on the rules and powers of select committees.

PROS

Although it is clearly difficult to get even chairs to confess to the weakness of some of their committee colleagues, committee officials seem to have no such problem. One in particular told me: 'This is a brilliant idea. The range in quality between different committees and individual inquiry sessions is stark.'

Bringing this additional level of rigour to the process would also make members really consider if they want to take part in a committee, rather than join and then contribute relatively little. We have to find a means of separating the passionate and committed from those who are going into it for the wrong reasons.

The compulsory nature of the programme would mean that MPs would not need to feel embarrassed about receiving training, and there is little doubt that providing this structured support would be of benefit to the quality of the committees' output. MPs should receive the type of support often paid for by corporates, which could be provided for by an increase in the budgets for the committees. This support would serve to focus the select committee members on their duties, but especially on how to get the most useful information from a witness to feed into the subsequent report.

Training in how to quiz and question witnesses could be provided as a special service by a leading barrister, or more generally by a law firm. It is likely that most law firms would be happy to be associated with one of the vital functions of Parliament, and provide that support on a reduced fees, or even *pro bono*, basis. The support would be general, rather than on specific committee inquiries, thus avoiding any conflicts of interest.

Even MPs themselves have identified that Parliament should be much less cautious about tapping into external expertise. As former Public Accounts Committee member (and subsequently Brexit Secretary) Steve Barclay MP notes: 'Our leading management business schools are just one talent pool which could assist select committees, where bright future leaders could undertake project work supporting members. It would inject some welcome fresh thinking.'[101]

CONS

In contrast, drilling and training MPs to think and act in set ways could only make the committees more robotic and crush the individual insights we would otherwise get from members' broad range of backgrounds.

There would also be a cost element for providing this training. But, more importantly, it could be argued that the varying levels of technique and expertise across the committees provides a more natural flow to proceedings. For all members to adopt the learned style of a barrister may be detrimental to the organic nature of the current committee hearings.

INCREASE ATTENDANCE

BACKGROUND

Data on the frequency of select committee hearings and the attendance rates of members is simply not available on Parliament's own website. Fortunately, the Institute for Government has crunched the numbers in its 2018 Parliamentary Monitor:

> Among the Commons departmental and cross-cutting committees in the year from the 2017 Queen's Speech, the Treasury Committee met most frequently (seventy-one times), and the International Trade Committee the least frequently (twenty-six times). The Treasury Committee's volume of meetings may reflect its role in scrutinising both the Treasury and HM Revenue and Customs, as well as overseeing appointments to other organisations such as the Bank of England's Monetary Policy Committee.[102]

Committees are therefore generally busy but one of the many frustrations expressed to me by select committee officials in particular was the poor attendance by certain members. Overall, Commons committee attendance averaged 72 per cent between June 2017 and June 2018 and, given the target cumulative attendance rate for members sits at 60 per cent, you may think this a cause of celebration. But if you missed on average three out of every ten major meetings with your boss, would you really be patted on the back? The difficulty in predicting which members will attend a select committee hearing has always been considered as discourteous to the witnesses, and it is unhelpful as the committee attempts to write its report based on information gleaned from the hearings.

In November 2009, the Wright Committee recommended that 'there should be clear consequences for unreasonable absence from select committees'.[103] Under his recommendations, to fit in with the proposed new system of elections, any member of a select committee whose cumulative attendance during a session is below 60 per cent would be automatically discharged at the end of that session on the basis of a report made by the Clerk of Committees to the Speaker.

PROPOSED SOLUTION

The Wright Committee's measures, although broadly seen as successful in transforming the effectiveness of the select committees, has still not solved the problem of poor attendance. Therefore, there should be a further tightening of the guidance, making select committee attendance compulsory unless an absence is agreed with the chair and communicated to the witnesses in advance. MPs who fall below a certain attendance level would need to explain in writing to the House why this has occurred, or could possibly even be fined.

Additionally, for the benefit of witnesses giving evidence, the committee should announce which members are able to attend any given session. Given the effort witnesses need to go to cancel other diary engagements, the least the committee can do is to alert them to whom they will be facing on the day.

PROS

Making select committee attendance compulsory, or increasing the number of members needed for a quorum (which is currently just three MPs or a quarter of the committee, whichever is the greater number) would prevent poor attendance, and may make an MP consider whether they have enough time before joining a committee. This sends a clear message that a select committee requires a significant commitment and time investment.

This move would also increase the quality of the committee's final reports and recommendations, as it would mean more of the MPs involved will have heard the oral evidence from witnesses first hand, and be far more engaged in the issue.

CONS

Failure to attend some select committee sessions does not automatically reflect laziness or lack of engagement. Being an MP is an incredibly demanding job, a fact which has been lost over a succession of expenses scandals, which caused such reputational damage to Parliament. If MPs are not present at a select committee hearing, it is most likely that they are undertaking an important function of their role representing their constituents. They have packed diaries and have to balance that with the competing needs in the Chamber itself, scrutinising important legislation.

As the Liaison Committee has noted, there can be other good reasons for lower attendance, such as personal or family illness, or regular diary clashes between a committee's meetings and a member's other parliamentary activities.

One current chair expressed their frustration at this criticism to me very strongly:

> It is not realistic for members to be on top of every issue because they simply don't have the time to spare. The public might not like to hear it, but MPs are vastly overworked. It is especially irritating to hear this call to cut down the number of MPs from 650 to 600. This is absolutely crazy, because it will damage the ability of Parliament to scrutinise. Being on a select committee means that MPs often have to neglect other things – whether it is their constituents, all party groups they may be on, as well as activities in the Chamber.

There are also times when individual MPs will bring to bear their specific strengths in a topic area and take a step back on others. For example, the MP may have a great deal of knowledge and expertise in the energy sector and thus commits to all the oral sessions related to this topic, but spends less time on a separate inquiry into gender pay gap ratios. By splitting roles in this way, colleagues on a select committee can still provide effective scrutiny but without duplicating their efforts for the sake of ticking an attendance box.

As the Institute for Government has calculated, the data for the year since the 2017 Queen's Speech shows that across the departmental and cross-cutting committees, the average 72 per cent attendance is well above the Liaison Committee target of 60 per cent and was up on the previous year's figure of 66 per cent, indicating that most committee members do take their responsibilities seriously.[104] If the trend shows an increase in committee attendance, then tougher measures may simply not be necessary.

BAN PARLIAMENTARY PRIVATE SECRETARIES FROM BECOMING SELECT COMMITTEE MEMBERS

BACKGROUND

A parliamentary private secretary (PPS) is appointed by a government minister to assist them in particular duties. They are selected from amongst backbench MPs to be the eyes and ears of the minister in the House of Commons. It is an unpaid responsibility, but it is deemed useful for an MP to become a PPS in order to gain experience of working in government. They are rather cruelly known as 'bag carriers' in and around Westminster, but the role has often been a stepping stone to a bigger job.

Although taking the route from PPS to the Cabinet is unusual (partly because an incoming government will often appoint senior ministers from the existing shadow team), many Cabinet members have served in this role, such as Amber Rudd and Gavin Williamson, and it is seen as a good grounding for becoming an actual minister. However, their close confidence with ministers does impose obligations on every PPS, and there are rigid guidelines surrounding the divulging of information to PPSs.

To that end, they are subject to some restrictions as outlined in the Ministerial Code. As things currently stand, a PPS can sit on a select committee but must avoid 'associating themselves with recommendations critical of or embarrassing to the Government',[105] and must not make statements or ask questions on matters affecting the minister's department. In particular, the PPS in the Department for Communities and Local Government may not participate in issues related to planning. Although MPs receive no extra money for the role, PPSs are expected to vote in line with the government on every decision and are regarded as members of the government for purposes of collective responsibility – they therefore must resign if speaking against government policy.

PROPOSED SOLUTION

The suggestion is that a PPS, especially one who reports in to a Secretary of State, should be prevented from serving on a select committee. This would effectively force anyone considering becoming a PPS to choose between the two roles.

Given that select committees are designed to help hold

government departments to account, it makes sense that government ministers are prohibited from membership of the standard select committees. After all, as a minister, you are obliged to vote with the government regardless of your own personal views. Even shadow ministers are often not permitted to become members of the same committees they shadow in their frontbench role. However, this interesting anomaly allows PPSs to serve on committees.

Having PPSs on committees can be problematic. They are often needed for departmental responsibilities which can clash with select committee sessions. They also have a responsibility to the government of the day, which leads to questions of impartiality when scrutinising a government department. As the Institute for Government has said, 'Despite the need for flexibility in the system, a resolution establishing the conventions about those ineligible to sit on committees would be useful.'

PROS

By excluding PPSs from select committees, we could entirely avoid some potential conflicts of interest and maintain the independence of the committees. The cynical view across Westminster and Whitehall is that the appointment of PPSs is just another means of expanding the government's numbers, to ensure loyalty with the promise of future advancement. Even more questionable is the allocation of a PPS to mid-level ministers of state, which I believe should be stopped completely – this would free a whole number of bright, newer MPs to become more engaged in the select committee process.

CONS

The PPS role can be an important function in developing a career in governing rather than simply scrutinising. As it is seen as the first step onto the ministerial ladder, forcing ambitious MPs to choose would make it less likely that they would remain on the select committee. This could have a detrimental impact on the ability of the committees to attract the best new talent, denying the committees good quality candidates who currently feel able to create a 'Chinese wall' between their dual responsibilities.

FORMALISE THE POWERS OF COMMITTEES REGARDING GOVERNMENT APPOINTMENTS

BACKGROUND

While select committees are expected to participate in the scrutiny of certain government appointments, they have no power to enforce their decision, in contrast to those in other countries, such as the US.

This was demonstrated clearly when the Digital, Culture, Media and Sport Committee challenged the appointment of Conservative peer Baroness Stowell as the new chair of the Charity Commission. She attended a hearing in Parliament, but the committee said it was 'unanimous' in its view that Stowell should not be appointed. It is the first time that this committee had not supported a government candidate.

In a letter to Matt Hancock, the then Secretary of State for Digital, Culture, Media and Sport, the committee said that it:

Could not support Stowell's appointment because of her lack of charity sector experience, concerns about her political neutrality, a lack of transparency in the recruitment process and because she failed to stand up to scrutiny when questioned by the committee ... her political past is a source of concern for the committee and those within the charity sector.[106]

However, before the select committee had even published its report on the matter, the Secretary of State had publicly announced that the government would continue with the appointment.

PROPOSED SOLUTION

Put simply, a unanimous objection from a departmental select committee on the appointment of a senior post of a public body should be binding.

PROS

The select committees should be viewed as having genuine powers, and not just as an informal shadow to the function of government departments. Properly equipping the committees with the right to object (as long as the verdict is unanimous) would make the government think much more carefully about listening to the concerns expressed. In the instance of Baroness Stowell, it was not just the opinion of the committee, but also a reflection of the views of many in the charity sector which would be governed by the new chair. To have ignored this in such a high-handed fashion was very poor conduct by the Secretary of State, and disrespectful to Parliament.

CONS

In an increasingly partisan Parliament, expanding the powers of the select committees to overrule government appointments is potentially dangerous, and could lead to pressure from chairs with a political axe to grind. This is especially the case where the chair is either from an opposition party or in dispute with their own side. Even where the verdict is not unanimous, the chair can still go to the media and garner significant coverage over their objections. Governments are there to make policy, and select committees to scrutinise. Implementing this change would disrupt this structure.

THE HEARING

ALLOW A BARRISTER TO LEAD
THE QUESTIONING

BACKGROUND

Although select committees can be gruelling for witnesses, the quality of the questioning can be entirely random and varies in quality from inquiry to inquiry. MPs get their ideas for questions from a range of sources, but most often from: the briefing pack put together by the committee's officials; research from their own parliamentary office; and their own existing prejudices or views about the person, company or issue. As a result, committees often fail to see the real issue at play and tend to miss open goals.

Even a current chair I interviewed admitted, 'I think witnesses being questioned by those who have not done their homework hands the advantage to the witness. I'm often so disappointed by how long it takes members to get to the point.'

On so many occasions, I have prepared senior people to anticipate what I consider to be the real (and seemingly obvious) killer questions which could unpick them, only to watch the committee focus instead on pointless minutiae, which allows the witness to remain in a relatively safe place.

Perhaps we should not be surprised. Cross-examining shrewd business professionals to extract key information is a real art and not something everyone can do naturally. It takes a barrister at least five years to become fully qualified. Is it any wonder, therefore, that MPs with a background in a trade union, nursing or insurance, for example, are not naturally adept at unpicking the global finance director of a multinational?

PROPOSED SOLUTION

Major committees should be allowed the use of a trained barrister to help the committee extract the maximum value from a session, especially a complex one. This was an idea very strongly suggested to me by one retired committee chair whom I interviewed. In their view, substandard questioning from amongst the committee members often let a key witness 'off the hook'. When combined with a lack of focus from the members (who often have not undertaken sufficient research of the issues) and time restrictions, the quality of the session falls. However, if a trained specialist were to support the committees by solely asking questions for the opening thirty minutes or so with a series of properly researched, laser-like questions to help build the key arguments, then the members would be able to hear the initial evidence, take notes and be ready to move in with the key supplementary questions for the remainder of the session.

PROS

The quality of scrutiny could be transformed, enhancing the reputation of the committees, helping to move away from lazy questions, such as 'How much are you paid?', towards those which truly illuminate the issue at hand. After the witnesses are cross-examined by a trained professional, most of the key facts will have been established and the members could then move in armed with better information, and therefore with a much clearer direction to follow for the remainder of the session. Taking a few steps back and watching proceedings more objectively would allow them to spot key inconsistencies or implausible answers. Given that a number of committee officials told me that one of their biggest frustrations is MPs turning up for hearings without having adequately prepared, this preamble could also act as a means of ensuring they understand the issue better prior to their involvement in the questioning.

The additional benefit is that simply working with a barrister and watching them in action would improve the technical abilities of select committee members, arguably making them more effective parliamentarians in the process.

CONS

Put simply, MPs on select committees are chosen, having been elected by voters, and lawyers are not. It would therefore be constitutionally challenging for a barrister to question a witness in Parliament without changes to the law. If we see Parliament as the democratic representative body of the people, then having an unelected private sector individual serving formally on a committee surely undermines its standing. This point was made by one particular chair I interviewed, who told me:

> This seems at best impracticable and at worst impossible. Select committees are made up of elected representatives who are then elected by the House; this is what gives them authority. If you foist outsiders upon us in this way, you are effectively saying we are not capable of representing our constituents.

For a witness to suddenly have to appear before a barrister, as well as just a group of MPs, would affect the dynamic dramatically. It is much more likely that witnesses, anxious not to incriminate themselves before someone with significant legal training, would be less forthcoming and would probably have to be permitted to have legal representation alongside them too. As things currently stand, bringing your legal representative onto the panel is seen as odd and reputationally damaging (it is very, very unusual) but should barristers join committees, future witnesses could justifiably request to have their own lawyer present.

Additionally, there could be conflicts of interest, even if the lawyer in question was only providing general help. They would gather significant knowledge about the motivations and interests of each of the committee members, gain privileged access to information and it would be incredibly difficult to track whether the lawyer's firm is exploiting its connection with the committee. It could be the next scandal waiting to happen. We already see this often when a barrister is appointed to lead an independent inquiry into a major catastrophe (e.g. in the aftermath of the terrible tragedy at Grenfell Tower) and questions are asked about why an individual may not be impartial.

As a final point, top barristers charge very significant hourly fees totalling many hundreds of pounds, which would mean Parliament would have to make a decision. Either it would need to fund this expensive resource, money which could be better spent in other areas, or the barrister would provide the service at a special or even *pro bono* rate. In that instance, questions around the motivations of the individual would plague their involvement throughout.

INTRODUCE TIME LIMITS TO QUESTIONS

BACKGROUND

Unlike US congressional committee hearings, our UK equivalents do not currently have any formal time limit to the individual contributions made by their members. It is therefore the responsibility of the committee's chair to manage proceedings as best they can to ensure members get a fair shot at asking their questions. These questions need to fit within the standard time frame for the majority of committee sessions, which tend to last between forty-five minutes and an hour. In some special cases, the oral sessions will run longer, but the committee still has to be mindful of the knock-on impact on any subsequent panels.

In many instances, the committee chairs are not success-ful in managing time effectively and one or two members can dominate proceedings, to the point where the sessions prove deeply unsatisfactory in terms of getting to the root of the issues.

PROPOSED SOLUTION

As such, we should end the unscientific and often random nature as to which members on a committee get to ask ques-tions and for what length of time. We should take the respon-sibility away from chairs of the committee, and instead assign a specific amount of time for questions to be asked. This would be a maximum of perhaps four minutes per question per member. The committee clerk or other senior official would either indicate to the chair how long was left so they could intervene, or a digital clock could be used so the person asking the question could see how long they had left to probe further.

PROS

Deploying this system would help to focus the minds of each select committee member to ensure they have worked harder in advance to produce a succinct set of questions, thus making each committee session as efficient as possible. MPs wishing to shine would have to prepare far more effec-tively to ensure they get straight to the point. It would also help to ensure that certain members do not dominate the questioning, thus allowing less publicity-minded members the same amount of airtime. For witnesses appearing before the committees, it would provide a clearer structure as to how the session will proceed, and they will know long answers to a specific line of questioning will not be permitted.

CONS

The lack of formal time limits is arguably one of the greatest weapons in a select committee's arsenal and allows it to deliver a greater level of scrutiny than those in the United States and elsewhere, which have to abide by set timings. It would undermine the authority of the committee chairs if they could no longer dictate the line of questioning due to an artificial structure.

Indeed, it would greatly advantage the witnesses giving evidence, who would be mindful that each member of the committee has a limited amount of time to question, and that would provide an opportunity to prevaricate until the time was up. As one chair told me, 'I don't like time limits to questions, because witnesses can game the system unless the questioners all combine and co-ordinate.' Additionally, there is real doubt as to whether such a rigid system would provide better outcomes in terms of the evidence which is uncovered. Often the best sessions occur when questions head in an unexpected direction, via an organic development of the discussion. Members are currently able to follow a line of inquiry until they get to an answer (or at least as close to an answer as is possible). It means that witnesses can't simply run down the clock and avoid scrutiny. The time taken for select committee sessions also varies dramatically, so implementing an arbitrary time limit in place across the board would be a poor policy.

There are real-life examples where the UK committee structure has been proven superior. In April 2018, the Digital, Culture, Media and Sport Committee took evidence from Facebook's chief technology officer Mike Schroepfer in its inquiry into fake news. Around the same time, the US Senate Judiciary and Commerce Committees held a joint session with the company's founder Mark Zuckerberg about the use of customer data. During the US hearing, Zuckerberg knew that each member had only four minutes to question him, so he consistently filibustered in order to avoid answering any tough questions. This was a luxury that Schroepfer was not able to enjoy, and the UK committee was widely considered to have gleaned more valuable information as a result.

END OR SUSPEND THE LIVE
BROADCASTING OF SELECT COMMITTEES

BACKGROUND

After the cameras were introduced in the main House of Commons chamber on 21 November 1989, many MPs believed it to be the beginning of the end for reasoned, sober debate.

The first person to speak on camera was the former Conservative MP Ian Gow (who was murdered by the IRA just six months later, by a bomb which, incidentally, I actually heard explode, as I lived nearby at the time). Mr Gow was a vociferous opponent of the introduction of cameras and made fun of this fact in his first address, when he made the following statement:

A letter that I received three weeks ago ... made the following preposterous assertion: 'The impression you make on television depends mainly on your image (55 per cent) with your voice and body language accounting for 38 per cent of your impact. Only 7 per cent depends on what you are actually saying.' ... The letter went on – and hon. Members may think that this is an extravagant claim so far as I am concerned: 'We can guarantee to improve your appearance through a personal and confidential image consultation. You will learn if you need a new hair style – and where to get it – and the type of glasses to suit your face.' The House will understand why I considered that I was beyond redemption on both counts.[107]

Mr Gow was bald and wore thick-rimmed glasses.

However, ambitious MPs soon grew to see personal benefits to having the cameras in the chamber. Knowing that a dramatic display could make the national news, many MPs on all sides were accused of hamming it up, not least during Prime Minister's Questions, the weekly opportunity to hold the Prime Minister to account in the House of Commons. Critics say the same thing has happened with the advent of select committees being filmed and screened on Parliament-Live and occasionally rolling news outlets. Suddenly, members were ever keener to deliver a media-friendly soundbite, as it might get them noticed.

The recording of select committees, some opponents claim, helps to lower the standard of proceedings and ultimately leads to a dumbing down of important inquiries. In comparison, they point to the less-publicised House of Lords hearings as evidence of how the system should work in the lower house – the peers are often more experienced and therefore past the point of needing to show off to the same extent, and arguably approach the sessions in a much more constructive manner.

One senior business leader told me that ending what he described as the 'televised kangaroo court' style of the hearings would radically improve their effectiveness. He suggested that the public argument is a weak one because the viewing figures for such sessions are very low, and those who do tune in are usually Westminster staff or other elite insiders. His suggestion is that all committee sessions take place without cameras, while still remaining open to the public and media. 'The cameras create the theatrics, and provokes MPs to play up,' he said. Perhaps it is time to reflect on whether the cameras are a help or a hindrance.

PROPOSED SOLUTION

The proposition, therefore, is that we should stop broadcasting select committee hearings, suspending the live feed as part of a six-month or year-long experiment to see whether it leads to a behavioural change from both the parliamentarians and the witnesses. After this review, an assessment can be made as to whether the committee process is seen to have improved as a result. I must report that this was one of the changes which elicited the starkest difference in attitudes between select committee chairs and the witnesses who appear before them. Let's face it: this issue ultimately exposes the self-interest of both groups.

PROS

Ending the filming of the sessions would encourage a more open discussion and debate of the issues at hand. This would, in turn, lead to better quality committee reports and therefore improve the policy-making process. It would take away much of the desire to showboat.

This decision would arguably make the most rapid difference to the culture of select committee sessions. Without an opportunity to create the killer soundbite for news programmes, MPs would be forced to focus more on the detail of the discussion and actually listen to the answers rather than feel obliged to unleash the clever phrases they may have spent days preparing in front of the mirror. I am convinced that you would get into a much more meaningful discussion about the areas of policy without cameras, and improving policy making is surely one of the basic functions of a select committee.

For the witnesses, the select committee process would become more structured and less pressurised. They would still be required to answer the questions posed to them, and it would still be transcribed, but they would not have to be as concerned about superficial considerations such as how they look, their body language and the humiliation from failing in front of an audience which could include family, friends and colleagues. This, in turn, could make a witness more willing to attend, including some of the big-name witnesses which some of the committees have failed to deliver in recent years, such as Dominic Cummings.

The idea that the public would be denied its opportunity

to watch the committee hearings is also debatable. In reality, these sessions are watched by those with a vested interest – for example, the media, political advisors or rival companies – rather than the average person in the street. Before you claim this is an affront to democracy and would cause widespread outrage, do you really believe that removing the cameras would be likely to lead to mass rioting?

CONS

The select committee chairs I put this to were united in opposition to this idea. Some even laughed out loud when I asked them, perhaps for good reason. As a number of them suggested, the public now expects to be able to see for themselves what happens in their seat of democracy, and to remove that right surely goes against the principles of openness which are required to build trust. The public may not choose to watch parliamentary proceedings very often, but they reserve the right to do so if they wish.

Parliament should be as transparent as possible. Select committees are the only form of scrutiny that organisations face by politicians that the public are able to see. Thousands of people do tune in every week to watch the proceedings of select committees, including members of the public who are interested in the specific area of discussion; professionals for whom the session is of great importance (e.g. investors, when the Governor of the Bank of England appears in front of the Treasury Committee); and, at times, victims who do not want to sit in the public gallery. Select committee reports can lead to controversial recommendations, and it is important that the public is given the greatest possible chance of understanding why and how those conclusions are reached.

Taking away the cameras allows the rich and powerful to escape being held to account by making it easier to rely on their transcribed words, learned by rote. Yes, the committee can still ask the witness how much they were paid or whether they will give back the monstrous bonus they were awarded, and the transcription of their answers may still be damning. But the cameras often pick out something else – a shifting of the body, a clearing of the throat, a refusal to make eye contact – all of which can tell us a great deal about the person being questioned. In short, removing the cameras makes it easier for dodgy people to get away with it.

I was reminded by one chair that there is actually no obligation for select committees to be televised, and if it was agreed by the committee (which could be at the insistence of a witness) then the proceeding may be held without cameras present. Select committees in the UK also have far stricter rules about the presence of the media in the room, compared with their equivalents in the United States, so there are ways of managing the experience in a way which can suit the witness. That said, this probably applies more to an expert witness than a CEO accused of wrongdoing.

There is also a practical consideration, in response to the (probably fair) assertion that 'normal' members of the public do not watch the hearings, and could choose to attend in person anyway. Westminster politics is already viewed as unrepresentative of the views and needs of the wider country, especially in regions several hours' travel from the capital. It would be deeply unfair to expect a member of the public who is genuinely interested in the debate to pay a significant sum of money to travel down from Newcastle or Carlisle to watch a one-hour hearing, when they can currently watch for free. It also arguably makes Parliament less relevant, at a time when there is already a significant challenge to the way politics is organised and conducted.

In summary, there is the potential to detrimentally impact one of the few positive perceptions the public has about the Westminster Parliament, namely our democratic representatives taking on the might of the billionaires or the furtive ministers, and winning. The footage of these battles can serve as a useful reminder of the values we hold dear and how no one should be too powerful to face the court of public opinion.

END THE USE OF CELEBRITY WITNESSES

BACKGROUND

Back in 1985, the US House Agriculture Committee tabled a hearing called 'The Plight of the Family Farmer'. This was, on the surface, a perfectly reasonable subject for that committee to examine. However, when the attendee list of expert witnesses for the evidence sessions was revealed, Washington watchers were somewhat surprised to see three major actresses – Jane Fonda, Sissy Spacek and Sally Field – pencilled in to inform the inquiry. The committee chair justified this on the basis that all three actresses had played farm wives in Hollywood movies.[108]

As politicians have become less and less popular in recent years, it is inevitable that they would find any means necessary to associate themselves with things and people who the public do like. This is not a new phenomenon, of course. Political parties have always loved winning celebrity endorsements, whether it was Margaret Thatcher with radio DJ and comedian Kenny Everett, Tony Blair with Oasis star Noel Gallagher or Jeremy Corbyn with grime artist Stormzy. The hope is that somehow some of the stardust from famous people can sprinkle onto them. In recent years, there have also been minor celebrity endorsements via 'task forces' cynically set up by political parties, such as ex-*Countdown* star Carol Vorderman advising the Conservatives on promoting maths literacy in schools.

Select committees do not need celebrity endorsements in the same way as political parties, but they have increasingly become wise to the publicity benefits that having such witnesses can deliver. Attention-seeking committee chairs have often decided to model their committee's own set-up on US congressional hearings, which have used celebrity witnesses for many years. When actor and lothario Russell Brand was invited to give evidence to the Home Affairs Committee about the rehabilitation of drug addicts (having written and spoken openly about his years of drug abuse), the chair, Keith Vaz, knew very well that it would result in a packed committee room and wall-to-wall coverage. As one chair wearily acknowledged, 'Russell Brand gets invited to talk about drug addiction because he will garner headlines for the committee.'

Here are examples of celebrity appearances, especially since committee chairs became elected by the whole House in 2010:

- Former Manchester United and England footballer Gary Neville gave evidence to the Digital, Culture, Media and Sport Select Committee on the proposed sale of Wembley Stadium in July 2018.[109]

- Russell Brand went before the Home Affairs Select Committee on 28 April 2012.[110] Total Politics provided a wonderfully acerbic sketch on his appearance:

  Brand is a witness that MPs won't forget in a hurry, who didn't bother even to wear a skinny tie over his vest during his evidence. The long raven-haired comedian gave the home affairs committee a very open account of his past drug addiction and recovery. Brand cracked jokes throughout, and when told that time was running out, he said, 'Time is infinite.' Adding, 'Who's next? Theresa May? She may not show up – check she knows which day it is.' Another corker was when he was given a dressing down and told 'it's not quite a Variety Show.' He retorted, 'You're providing a little variety though. Making it more like *Dad's Army*.'[111]

- Movie stars Hugh Grant and Steve Coogan (as well as

the former president of Formula 1 Max Mosley) gave evidence to the Joint Committee on Privacy and Injunctions in December 2011.[112] Speaking out against media intrusion of privacy and on gagging injunctions, the trio gave colourful evidence. Grant told the committee he was there 'for the country, if that doesn't sound too pompous'. Coogan said that papers should issue front-page apologies, which Mosley said wouldn't have helped his case. He added that privacy is different, and if the *News of the World* had printed 'it was a private orgy' on their front page in apology, 'that wouldn't have helped me'.

- Mary Portas, star of BBC Two's *Mary, Queen of Shops*, gave evidence to the Communities and Local Government Select Committee's inquiry into the future of the high street in September 2013.[113]

- Celebrity chef Jamie Oliver is one of the favourites of the Health Committee, having appeared in both 2015 and 2018, as he is still seen to be popular and he loves a good soundbite. He gave evidence on the obesity crisis amongst children and argued in favour of a sugar tax on fizzy drinks.

These witnesses are also often given the most sycophantic treatment by the committees in awe of their brilliance (and often in return for a selfie for their social media sites) as part of an informal, presumably unspoken, agreement for them to appear in the first place.

PROPOSED SOLUTION

Although this would only be a voluntary system, there should be pressure on chairs of select committees to demonstrate that the witnesses they have invited to appear are genuinely the most qualified experts available. In the examples I have mentioned above, that was simply not the case. The media, rather than being equally star-struck, should be naming and shaming the celebrity love-ins and holding the committees to account.

If we want to demonstrate the authority of our committee system, then in every instance we need to see that the chairs are doing their utmost to maintain the integrity of the position they fill.

PROS

Conservative MP Michael Gove may have infamously declared during the 2016 EU referendum that 'people in this country have had enough of experts', but this should not be the approach taken by our parliamentary committees. The use of celebrity witnesses is damaging the standing of the select committees, in the sense that they may be perceived as dumbing down the importance of the evidence being received.

Can we not do better when looking for a specialist to talk about child obesity than a TV chef? Can we not find someone more apt to talk about the future of our national stadium than a retired footballer? Can we not find someone more appropriate to explain the challenges of addiction to hard drugs than a millionaire celebrity who has potentially made drug misuse seem cool?

Cutting out the celebrity witnesses would restore a level of respect to the select committee system, ensuring that the correct people with the right knowledge are appearing in any given inquiry.

CONS

The strongest argument returns to the overall point about the modern select committee structure, namely that by making the process more accessible, the more likely it is that you can engage the public and highlight the good work being done by parliamentarians. If it takes Jamie Oliver, with his millions of fans, to highlight the important work of the Health Committee, then perhaps that is a price worth paying.

The appearance of openly gay rugby referee Nigel Owens in the inquiry into homophobia in sport hugely increased the profile of that important inquiry, which would have been magnified further if the same committee had been successful in persuading Olympic diver Tom Daley to appear.

The inclusion of celebrities is also sometimes difficult to avoid. The Digital, Culture, Media and Sport Committee's inquiry into pay at the BBC was focused largely on big household names and whether their pay was proportionate at a time when the licence fee seemingly continues to lose popularity. It may have seemed odd that evidence was given by BBC radio presenter Liz Kershaw, but she gave very important evidence of how her employer had allegedly coerced her into setting up a 'personal service company', which caused her great personal financial difficulties.[114]

There is also an issue in terms of defining who is and who

is not a celebrity. For example, TV presenters and authors such as Richard Dawkins and Sir David Attenborough would probably be considered celebrities if they were spotted walking down the high street. Yet, Dawkins is an emeritus fellow of New College, Oxford, and was the University of Oxford's Professor for Public Understanding of Science, while Attenborough is a globally recognised natural historian of significant repute.

WIDER GOVERNMENT ISSUES

FORCE GOVERNMENT TO
RESPOND MORE QUICKLY

BACKGROUND

Measuring the impact of select committees on government policy is difficult. Just adding up all the committee recommendations which government accepts is one method, but can be highly misleading. A committee may recommend something which the government already thinks is a good idea, but is that as powerful as a committee report which is broadly rejected but changes the nature of the policy debate? The fact that a committee is already taking a keen interest in a topic can also jolt the government into pre-emptive action, for which the committee may not receive credit.[115]

Committee scrutiny can also have an indirect influence by forcing departments to review neglected policy areas and assess how they collect data. The very fact that government has to respond to each inquiry report emphasises the unique ability of the committees to pull the levers of government.

It is also useful to consider how government departments are performing against their mutually agreed sixty-day target for reply.

Thanks to analysis from the Institute for Government, we know the following:

- The government took an average of seventy-five days to respond to Commons reports, clearly breaching the agreed time frame.

- The Science and Technology Committee had the quickest government responses to their reports, taking just thirty-six days on average. The Exiting the EU Committee also received relatively speedy responses, in an average of fifty-four days.

- The government responded most slowly to reports published by the Justice Committee, taking 103 days on average. The Health and Social Care and Transport departments were also particularly slow to respond.

The data indicates that the government responded to sixty-two committee reports in the twelve months from the state opening of Parliament in June 2017.

Of these responses, 30 per cent were received within the Government's target timeframe of sixty days. The only committees which received a 100 per cent response within sixty days from their departments were International Trade, and Science and Technology. At the opposite end of the spectrum, the Work and Pensions, Transport, Scottish Affairs and Health and Social Care Committees did not receive a response to any of their reports within the sixty-day time limit, raising questions about the timeliness of government's responses.[116]

PROPOSED SOLUTION

Parliament should set a time limit for government responses to select committee reports, which moves away from the current loose advisory setting of sixty days. Instead, there should be a formal agreement, as well as the introduction of new sanctions for departments that fail to respond within the time frame. The relevant Secretary of State would have to write to the committee chair within twenty-four hours of missing the deadline, with a full explanation as to why his or her department has failed to meet the sixty-day target, and potentially that minister and their senior officials (preferably the Permanent Secretary) would then be hauled before the relevant committee within a week in order to explain in person why the deadline was missed.

PROS

This measure relates to the overall desire to afford the select committees the necessary powers and respect to keep them relevant and effective. The committee chairs I spoke with said this tougher line on government departments would be very helpful, as their failure to adhere to the recommended time frame is a growing problem and hampers the speed at which inquiries can be completed and progressed. This formal pressure would ensure that the government responds in a more timely fashion, not least because the relevant minister and senior official will not want to face another hostile session to explain the inefficiencies of their own department.

To use the infamous campaign slogan from the Leave campaign, this would be a means of the select committees 'taking back control' and show the country that their work is of supreme importance.

CONS

Select committee reports can be significant in size and depth and sometimes it is not feasible to respond within the allotted time frame. As one senior official told me, in a department shadowed by a very active select committee, 'We are already stretched. There are numerous parliamentary "events" to prepare for and respond to, exacerbated by the work we have to do on Brexit, and with a smaller headcount of people each year. The select committees cannot expect miracles!'

The sixty-day limit should remain an advisory measure to ensure the government is able to provide the right responses, not just the quickest. Given the length of time it takes for legislation to pass, it is not unreasonable that responding to a sizeable report also takes time.

MINIMISE IMPACTS OF
A GENERAL ELECTION

BACKGROUND

A general election, by definition, disrupts the political process. As soon as the election is called, Parliament is dissolved and all 650 seats become vacant. Once the election is completed, the losing MPs are turfed out of their offices, their possessions packed away and the office keys taken back. It can be a brutal and traumatic process for the MPs involved, especially where they had not believed defeat to be likely.

Select committees also have to stop their investigations and hearings as soon as Parliament is dissolved, which means that the chairs and members are effectively no longer on the committee, and in some instances may not return if they are defeated. The time then taken to re-establish committees means that elections create significant gaps in Commons committees' scrutiny of government.

The June 2017 general election was especially disruptive for the select committee system. The election was called by the Prime Minister on 18 April, with Parliament dissolved on 3 May. This meant that the committees were not functioning in any real way from the announcement date all the way through to the post-conference return on 9 October, which demonstrates how jarring snap elections are to the process of select committee scrutiny. The Liaison Committee was not established until 6 November and did not choose its chair and begin to exercise its functions under various standing orders until 13 November.[117] By convention, the Liaison Committee is the only committee that can take oral evidence from the Prime Minister, which meant there was a gap of a year before the first evidence session in the 2017 parliament. Given the unique challenges of Brexit, it is extraordinary that the Prime Minister could go so long without select committee scrutiny of her policies.

The slow speed in re-establishing Commons committees following an election is a democratic problem because it creates a gap in the scrutiny of government, which it has no real incentive to fix. Many live inquiries were brought to a premature end by the 2017 general election, and many new areas of inquiry simply missed their moment.

The Institute for Government has calculated that:

Out of the 300 Commons committee inquiries underway when the election was called, 100 had to be left unfinished. The remainder were curtailed prematurely, with committees rushing the publication of reports and evidence before the House was dissolved and they ceased to exist. The government also avoided having to respond to some of the 122 inquiry reports that were awaiting a response when the election was called.[118]

The unsatisfactory nature of this situation was highlighted by the Commons Procedure Committee, which launched an inquiry into establishing select committees in a new Parliament, in summer 2018. The committee had not reached its conclusions at the time of going to print, but it has already noted the 'substantial disquiet inside and outside the House over the perceived delay in establishing departmental and other select committees and the apparent lack of committee scrutiny of the Government's actions'.[119] The Procedure Committee's inquiry will examine whether further changes to the system need to be made.

PROPOSED SOLUTION

The selection of select committee chairs and members needs to be seen as an absolute priority for the parliamentary authorities. A provision could be made to compel the tabling of the motion to allocate the chairs in a shorter timescale, setting an explicit limit of one week instead of the current two. Neil Parish, the chair of the Environment, Food and Rural Affairs Committee has suggested that 'departmental select committees should be established no more than four weeks after State Opening and/or no more than two weeks after the election of Committee Chairs'.[120] There may also be a case for implementing a shadow committee team, formed of the members of the committee prior to the dissolution of Parliament, to provide temporary scrutiny while the actual committee is formed.

PROS

The delay in appointing committee members has affected the reputation of committees. It is simply unacceptable that almost half a year went by in 2017 without select committee scrutiny of government policy, especially given the turmoil of Brexit. The government needs to be held to account throughout the year, not just when Parliament can get its act together. By getting the committees up and running more speedily, they can get back to their vital work. If investigations by committees could have taken place earlier, they would then have been more likely to inform debate on a variety of issues, such as the Grenfell Tower disaster.

There were also business leaders who escaped having to answer for their activities during this period, because an event in June would have been long forgotten by the October/November return of the committees.

In 2017, the widely accepted reason for the delay came from the fact that the government did not have a clear majority, leading to significant haggling over membership of committees. Given that the past three general elections have produced either a hung parliament or a very small government majority, we must assume that these challenges will continue. We cannot, then, remain complacent about the way we reconstitute the committees.

As was pointed out by Dr Marc Geddes of Edinburgh University, some committees also have responsibilities beyond the conduct of scrutiny, such as the scheduling of business in the chamber or in Westminster Hall – notably the Backbench Business Committee, Petitions Committee and Liaison Committee. Delaying their establishment means that Parliament was not fully functioning until long after the general election in June 2017.[121]

There was also a bizarre situation in which chairs were elected, but the wider membership of the committee was not established, thus meaning they were able to make pronouncements on behalf of a non-existent committee.

CONS

There are some benefits to not electing chairs in haste. In 2010, the party split of chairships were allocated three weeks after the general election, with nominations closing two weeks later. Elections took place one day after the close of nominations. In 2015 and 2017, there was approximately a week between the close of nominations and the ballot, which allowed candidates to campaign and circulate election literature. This approach arguably made these elections for chairships more competitive, and allowed newly elected MPs time to learn about candidates.

Furthermore, we are assuming that Parliament is purposely dragging its heels in terms of reconvening the committees, when in fact the delay may simply be a reflection of the scale of the challenge the parliamentary authorities face when Parliament is dissolved and then reconstituted after a general election. There are numerous processes to oversee, and select committees have to fit within them. In the instance of 2017, the return after the election was short, just over a month, before the summer break when Parliament is in recess. Then, on return, there is only two weeks before it breaks again for the party conference season. Parliament can only work with the limited time and resources it has.

CONCLUSION

Periodic review of the select committee system is an important way of ensuring that it remains relevant. With both the House of Commons and the House of Lords undertaking reviews of its respective systems, it is hoped that some of the ideas above will be considered as part of that process.

Admittedly, none of the proposed solutions I have explored provides a single, easy hit which will solve all the current challenges, but there are elements which could be implemented to significantly improve the way our select committees work.

I would be strongly in favour of strengthening the powers of the select committees to compel witnesses to appear, regardless of the admittedly tricky issues this would create. The current system is too opaque and does not therefore help the reputation and standing of the committees. Giving committee chairs the real legal muscle to compel a witness who otherwise has no reasonable argument for not appearing would radically empower them.

Of course, some committee chairs could abuse those powers by hauling in all and sundry to an inquiry session, but we already have an unsatisfactory scattergun system. We may as well give the chairs some added heft to get the right people to give evidence, and trust them to not take advantage of the new freedoms this would provide.

I also think it is game, set and match in the debate as to whether select committees should receive additional financial and training resources to function more effectively. There are such significant benefits to having strongly performing select committees to improve public policy and to challenge wrongs in wider society. We should prioritise this and fund the system properly. Let us give committees the money required to train MPs to the best possible standard, to get the best external support of specific inquiries, to attract the best talent to work for the committees and to make the system much more effective for the people it represents.

There are not many other walks of life where roles of such huge importance and responsibility are provided to people utterly unprepared for the technical skills required to carry them out. This, by the way, extends to many other aspects of Parliament and government. It is preposterous that departmental briefs in the Cabinet are often foisted onto people with little to no understanding of the topic they are representing. For instance, the Secretary of State for Northern Ireland, Rt Hon. Karen Bradley MP, admitted that she did not know that nationalists and unionists in the region did not vote for one another, before coming under intense pressure to resign for suggesting that 'over 90 per cent of the killings during the Troubles were at the hands of terrorists ... the fewer than 10 per cent that were at the hands of the military and police were not crimes'.[122] The Secretary of State for Digital, Culture, Media and Sport, Rt Hon. Jeremy Wright MP, admitted that he is not tech savvy, does not subscribe to a single newspaper and was caught out pretending to like sport.[123] Jobs in politics are often dished out not by matching talent to a position, but based on the seniority of the role. By providing MPs with properly structured training and investing in their skills, we could get so much more from our select committees, making them better at holding the powerful and influential to account. It might also help to prepare them for life outside of Parliament given the current volatile nature of British politics.

Furthermore, we have every right to expect MPs to actually show up and prioritise their role on a select committee. In any other career, it would not be considered acceptable to pitch up for meetings on six out of every ten occasions. I would be very supportive of much stricter rules to ensure that the committees are properly populated for each and every oral evidence session. Related to this issue of commitment to being on a select committee, I am not, however, convinced that banning PPSs from serving on committees is a sensible idea. We should be trying to encourage the next generation of MPs to develop their skills of both governing and scrutinising, and forcing them to choose Parliament over party at such an early stage would seem counterproductive.

I am taken by the idea of regional select committees, at least on a trial basis. Increasingly, we need to find ways to connect local communities who feel alienated by the processes in Westminster, and this would be at least a move in the right direction. The reports provided by regional committees would be important to those communities, even if the national media showed little interest in covering them.

This would also likely expand one of the benefits of select committees reported by numerous interviewees, namely the camaraderie which often develops across party lines. One chair told me, 'I do a lot of cross-party work on key issues, and that willingness to do this stems from being a select committee chair. It taught me how to do it and understand people from other political sides.'

It is amazing that otherwise political enemies can serve alongside one another and develop a mutual respect by working together on an issue of mutual interest. I heard that view expressed several times about former Public Accounts Committee chair, Dame Margaret Hodge MP, who garnered significant affection from right-wing Conservative MPs serving under her. Imagine how beneficial it would be for MPs from regions with a mix of party political persuasions to examine local issues, not through the prism of bitter electoral considerations but through common purpose.

Ideally, regional committees should be combined with a more thematic approach. For example, transport issues are examined by the Welsh Select Committee for transport issues in Wales, the Transport Committee for England, the Public Accounts Committee regarding their value for money and other committees at the level of European scrutiny. Committees rarely speak to each other to leverage evidence and expertise; as a result, officials can constantly change the goalposts.

I am most troubled by the idea of a barrister being introduced into select committee hearings as a means of interrogating the witnesses. I do accept that they have abilities to cross-examine in a way most MPs do not, but it would be best for barristers to provide those skills as part of MP training, rather than to have a specific role themselves. To do so would undermine the right of democratically elected representatives who are ultimately accountable to the British people. Outsourcing the questioning would make many wonder what the role of the MP is, just as we have seen with the rise of policy measures seeking to take political decision making out of the hands of our politicians (such as the setting of interest rates by the Bank of England).

Furthermore, time-limited questions for members would, in my view, prevent a session from developing organically. Setting a time measure would not, in itself, lead to better questions. The key is to focus on improving the research and preparation of MPs to aid the quality questioning, rather than worry about the time frame in which those questions are asked.

In terms of switching off the television cameras, I think the genie is long out of the bottle and is never going to go back in. Yes, the public does not tend to sit around during the daytime idly watching select committee hearings online, but that is not really the point. The public should have the opportunity, should they wish, to see for themselves the important work of Parliament being conducted before the cameras. There is already the option of providing private evidence in some instances, and I fear that banning the live footage would only help the witnesses that we need to answer important questions about policy or business practices which affect us most.

The ending of celebrity appearances is admittedly not a priority but I do take the point that sensible, expert opinion is undermined by this increase in publicity-seeking witness chasing. We need the committees to invest their time in finding the right people, regardless of whether they will be a draw for the media or for members of the public. I think in essence, this is about committee chairs exercising some caution around whether they are inviting a witness for the right reasons, or whether they have compromised on the quality of the evidence in return for getting a selfie with one of their heroes.

However, requiring the government to respond much more quickly to reports published by a select committee should be a high priority. I think the public would be shocked to discover how regularly certain departments fail to provide a response within sixty days. It smacks of a disregard for the committee system, and more widely a disregard for the policy challenges those committees rightfully make. This also relates to the issue around the right for select committees to unanimously reject a government appointment to a public body. It cannot be acceptable for a Secretary of State to make a decision in the face of such opposition in Parliament.

By implementing a number of these changes proposed to me during the course of my research, we can strengthen and empower the committees. One chair told me that he remained optimistic about the future: 'My prediction is that committees will become more activist in their work. I think eventually committees will become the key body to scrutinise legislation, not just shadow the process.'

If select committees can develop in this way, we will make them better trusted by the public, more attractive to join and more effective at holding the government and others in positions of power to account.

PART 3

A SURVIVOR'S GUIDE

Confessions of a select committee witness

Before we get stuck into what you must do to survive a select committee, I want to begin with a sobering account prepared for me by a senior executive who had to undergo several high-profile hearings during his tenure at a FTSE 100 company, and who understandably wished to remain anonymous:

I know it will seem like sour grapes, but having experienced a number of gruelling sessions in the course of my career, I have concluded that the select committee process serves nobody given the way in which it is conducted, especially over the past decade.

Major company executives should, of course, be held to account, but the constant attempt to humiliate them should stop. It has become similar to a weird form of medieval torture. What makes it worse is that I know my family, friends, colleagues and bosses all watch – so the pressure is horrendous. I would say at a minimum it takes at least two full days out of my working calendar and eight days of others' time to help gather data.

Let's just be honest and say that the select committees are not trying to get to the truth – at least, not a full understanding of what actually happened and how things work in the private sector. I've never felt that getting to the truth was ever the aim of these sessions.

On most of the occasions in which I appeared, it was clear that the select committee chair had written his or her closing remarks prior to the beginning of the session. How is that an indication that the committee approaches its inquiries with an open mind, or any level of balance?

The cameras do not help. They create the theatrics and help to make it like a cheap American TV court drama. There is no discussion; it is relentless political point scoring. Given the environment is so toxic, it makes me super careful about what I say, rather than explore policy in a way which could ultimately make government and business work more effectively.

The MPs make it abundantly clear that they are all out to get you. For example, questions on individual pay are just not fair unless taxpayer money is involved. Why is it anyone's business what a private company pays its people?

The whole objective is therefore not to blow it. It is never about winning because that is impossible – it is about survival.

INTRODUCTION

Parts 1 and 2 have demonstrated that the select committees we have today are largely as a result of Parliament's incremental attempts to tinker with their structure. Despite notable improvements since the last major reforms of 2010, the committee system remains flawed. In the absence of committees which fully meet our expectations, they often choose to adopt a style which is designed to paper over their faults, by creating moments of great drama. This theatre attempts to place you centre stage, not as the hero, but as the tragic figure, doomed to fail. In this final section, I want to show you how to survive the slings and arrows of a committee hearing.

So, let us imagine that you have received the dreaded request from a select committee to appear. How do you ensure that you emerge from your appearance with your reputation intact?

I have been involved in the training of senior executives for more than 100 separate select committee inquiries, and during that time I have identified the best possible ways of ensuring success. It is my belief that anyone can be trained and prepared to deliver a performance before a select committee which protects not only their personal reputation, but also that of the organisation they represent. That said, it is unsurprising that some people start with certain inbuilt advantages. I would define them as:

- Experience: when the witness knows far, far more than the committee's members about a topic, it is less likely that they will be caught out. That is why I suggest egos must be put to one side to ensure the best-equipped witness is put forward. One great example from my previous training was Jerry Petherick, who is responsible for running several major prisons on behalf of G4S, which had been unpopular with a number of select committees. His company may have been in the firing line, but Jerry has nearly forty years' experience in the prisons system, including as a governor. When he gave evidence, the committee could not help but warm to him and listen carefully to his explanation of how challenging prison management can be. In a word, he was authentic, and committees cannot help but be impressed by such witnesses.

- Eloquence: the ability to communicate well is not necessarily enough on its own, but politicians recognise the same abilities which are valued in their own profession. When a witness is able to explain a complex problem in a clear way, they will always get a more favourable response from a committee.

- Charisma: the select committees take evidence from a lot of dull people. In fact, the committee itself may well be filled with dull people. When a witness has charisma, it becomes easier to be persuasive, even if the message they are delivering is not especially welcomed. As an example, the current CEO of outsourcer Serco (and also the grandson of Sir Winston Churchill), Rupert Soames, represents a company frequently in trouble with political audiences, and yet always manages to win their respect through his natural charm.

Regardless of whether the people I have trained had all or any of these qualities, I have been fortunate in being able to prepare them successfully. In just a couple of instances, I have had senior witnesses who were very resistant to training and their performances suffered significantly as a result.

However, let us start with the basics of the process, and what you need to do to get ready.

HOW TO PREPARE

PRE-ANNOUNCEMENT

Generally speaking, most select committee inquiries, especially those which are considered as a reaction to a major news event, should not come as a surprise to the people compelled to appear.

For example, Company X has had its customer credit card records hacked. Company Y has had to cancel its entire flight schedule because of snow, leaving thousands of passengers stranded. Company Z is found to have paid zero tax on revenues of £1 billion and a journalist has written an in-depth story exposing this fact.

All these instances should have already sparked concern within a company that one of the relevant select committees will take an interest. If it is genuinely blindsided, it does not bode well for its chances of success.

From speaking to a number of committee chairs both past and present, the means by which these stories attract their attention tends to vary. Sometimes the story will simply be the front-page lead for their paper of choice (or in the cuttings gathered by the committee's officials); sometimes it will be caused by a journalist calling and asking if the news story will be investigated by the committee (which puts pressure on them to act); or often colleagues will approach them on the parliamentary estate and suggest that an inquiry is absolutely essential.

Although I do not want to paint a picture of a wholly calculated and cynical decision-making process, it is inevitable that in the current 24/7 rolling news culture, committee chairs will often be reactive. This, incidentally, highlights the need to try to see off potential knee-jerk inquiries by handling and managing your corporate crisis in the right way, as your immediate responses will be closely scrutinised for any evidence of complacency, denial or senior executives seen to be going missing. This could be the topic of a whole other book, so I will not deal with it here in any great detail, but every company should have a plan in place in case of crisis. It is staggering how few companies I meet have one.

Quite often, a committee chair will be caught on the spot with a news story at a time when a wider discussion with the other committee members, or even committee officials, has not been possible (for example, during parliamentary recesses). In those instances, the chair may end up making it clear to the media that an inquiry is likely to be forthcoming, but with a cleverly worded phrase which gives them a way out if required.

For instance, the initial response from the chair might be, 'I am very disappointed to see the way company X has behaved, and I shall be watching very closely over the next few days because it is possible my committee may need to speak to the chief executive to get the answers his customers are seeking.' Or the chair could say that the committee will be writing to the chief executive in an open letter to demand answers. Either way, the committee is not actually obliged to hold an oral session, but it is demonstrating that it is fulfilling its role as a watchdog.

As and when the committee does meet for its (usually) weekly session, there will be a number of longer-term topics to be discussed – for example, an inquiry into future pensions provision or social care for the elderly – but alongside those subjects will often be much more instant 'newsy' items. The committee members will then need to decide amongst themselves, guided by the chair, whether to make time in a busy schedule to hold a special session. The reality is that most committees will take on a mix of topics, effectively cross-subsidising the longer-term, yet less glamorous inquiries with a few headline grabbers to keep the media, public and colleagues happy.

Once an inquiry launch is agreed, the committee's officials will begin working up the parameters of the session and contacting the target companies or individuals who will be crucial to (hopefully) providing the answers to the committee's questions.

FORMAL ANNOUNCEMENT

When a select committee decides to push ahead with an inquiry, it will put out a press release to announce that it has been launched. This is usually sent to all those on the committee's mailing lists (including the relevant media), as well as posted on the committee's website (which is hosted on the main Parliament website) and on social media channels, such as Twitter. The press release, complete with a quote from the chair, may also manage to feed into ongoing media coverage of the news story; at least, this is what the committee is hoping, because they are all hungry for publicity.

Let us take a recent example to demonstrate how the savvy select committee operates. During the summer of 2018, Rachel Reeves, the impressive chair of the Business, Energy and Industrial Strategy Committee, sat patiently while the debate around the market shares of the so-called Big Four accountancy firms (EY, KPMG, Deloitte and PwC) heated up following a number of auditing scandals, such as Carillion and British Home Stores (BHS). A number of inquiries were called, most notably from the Competition and Markets Authority (now chaired by former Treasury Committee chair Andrew Tyrie) and a government review into the effectiveness of the audit regulator, the Financial Reporting Council.

Rather than dash into a knee-jerk response and be accused of jumping on an already heavily loaded bandwagon, Reeves met privately with a few of the audit firms. It appeared initially that she might decide to keep the committee out of this particular issue. However, she later agreed to do a keynote speech at one of the professional bodies which represent the audit industry and used that platform to announce a major inquiry into the audit market.

This is the tweet that announced the launch of the inquiry:

Business, Energy and Industrial Strategy Committee
@CommonsBEIS Nov 12

Today at @ICAEW Chartered Accountants Hall our Chair
@RachelReevesMP launched our inquiry into the future of the
#audit market. The text of speech here https://www.parliament.
uk/business/committees/committees-a-z/commons-select/
business-energy-industrial-strategy/news-parliament-2017/
future-audit-inquiry-speech-17-19/

By not jumping in when the other inquiries were announced, Reeves was able to find the time and space to seize the initiative. Using the keynote speech opportunity, with a captive audience of journalists and industry figures, Reeves was able to achieve maximum impact across all major newspapers and broadcast media. This was much more effective than simply uploading a press release to the website.

Here were some of the headlines that greeted her speech:

- 'MPs join rush to investigate "broken" British audit market', *The Times.*
- 'MPs to probe audit market over fears accounts resemble "works of fiction"', *Daily Telegraph.*
- 'Angry MPs challenge regulators over BHS', *Scottish Daily Mail.*
- 'MPs launch inquiry into future of "broken" audit sector', *City AM.*

Reeves cleverly ensured that she tapped into existing media

interest in the issue, and used it as a means to boost coverage of her own committee's activities. Just as an aside, it is amusing how the media chooses to portray MPs, depending on the issue. For instance, most of the time the media likes to suggest that our parliamentary representatives are deceitful, slippery crooks, and/or just ineffective. Yet when it suits them, such as a select committee examining a sector which they think is doing wrong, a bunch of MPs are transformed into supercharged, heroic representatives of the people.

Whatever the issue, following the announcement of an inquiry, relevant companies, trade bodies and government officials should be on high alert for a potential approach from a committee.

WRITTEN EVIDENCE

Once an inquiry has been announced and launched, the committee must then encourage the submission of written evidence from members of the public and affected organisations, and provide a deadline for receipt of that evidence. The time frame for this can range between a few days and several weeks, and the volume of documentation they receive is surprisingly high.

According to the Institute for Government, in the year following the 2017 Queen's Speech:

Commons committees opened a total of 409 inquiries …
On average, each Commons committee report received

44 pieces of written evidence and drew on oral evidence from 12 oral witnesses ... Volume of evidence is not in itself a measure of the quality of an inquiry, but a high volume of written evidence can reflect public interest in the subject of an inquiry.

However, despite the thirst for written evidence, it can be dispiriting for witnesses to realise how infrequently their submissions are seemingly read and absorbed by the MPs, although the officials do obviously try to blend the key points into the briefing materials for committee members.

In terms of the structure of the written evidence, the committees also like you to state clearly who the submission is from, i.e. whether it is sent by you in a personal capacity or on behalf of an organisation. This will just highlight that the submission is: 'Written evidence submitted by [name], [job title] at [company name]'.

You will not be surprised to discover that most calls for written evidence get only a limited response from very interested parties and specialists in any given area, but occasionally a topic will be so high-profile that a committee is inundated with submissions. Given the potential for these to be made by a range of pressure groups or other third parties, it makes sense to be concise – the website generally suggests a maximum of 3,000 words. Occasionally, the committee will specify more or fewer words in the inquiry terms of reference, but just use common sense. They will not punish you for being a bit over, but if you cannot sum up your arguments in 3,000 words then you are probably not trying hard enough. The job of reading them all is taken on by the committee's officials and the evidence will form part of the briefing pack they prepare for their committee.

The document should then begin with an executive summary in bullet-point form outlining the main points made in the submission. You can probably guess that this is the bit that all committee officials will definitely read, whereas your dense text with footnotes may not be so easily absorbed. The executive summary must therefore be really strong, clear and concise and set out what you want people to know. It is the equivalent of what is often called an 'elevator pitch', where if you only had thirty seconds to outline your views on a topic, you should have no more than three to five clear messages to deliver.

Your written evidence should include a brief introduction about yourself/your organisation. This should not go on for too long, but it is a great opportunity to get across some key facts about your organisation, for example: 'We are the UK's second biggest employer of 18–24-year-olds'; 'We have offices in all major UK cities, including Birmingham, Newcastle and Manchester'; or 'We have the lowest gender pay gap in our sector'. Think really hard about what makes you stand out, but also what it is about your company that MPs might see as fitting with their agenda. Just making lots of money for investors is, sadly, no longer sufficient.

You also need to present your reason for submitting evidence – and no, saying 'because you forced us to' is not a smart response. It always pays to flatter the committee to some extent, reflecting on the importance of the committee's investigation. If you are in the firing line then everyone knows that you do not really want to be in contact with the select committee at all, but this is all something of a game and you need to play it. Companies that are the focus of an issue being examined do not tend to choose to send in a submission proactively; they are often forced to by the committee as part of an inevitable drift towards giving oral evidence.

The real opportunity is for people or organisations which are trying to make a policy point which they want Parliament, and often the public at large, to know. So, for example, you may want to highlight one of the ghastly secondary ticketing firms that rip off music fans. This will be a big opportunity for consumer groups, such as Which?, to highlight the sector's often appalling practices and, in some cases, use it as a springboard for a so-called super complaint. This can be made by a government-designated consumer group and requires the regulator to publicly respond within ninety days to confirm whether it believes that there is an issue to investigate. Where there is, the regulator must set out what further steps it intends to take. Encouraging a select committee to launch an inquiry around the same time puts significant pressure on regulators, such as the Competition and Markets Authority, to act.

Although Parliament has always been behind the curve on digital engagement, the standard means of making a submission to a committee is via the online portal on the relevant inquiry page of the committee's website. The portal includes a basic form to record the contact details of those submitting evidence and is reasonably user-friendly, if a little dated. However, if you have been in contact with a particular official on the committee, it is also just as likely you will be able to send a standard email to him or her with your written evidence attached.

The committee format requests that any documentation you email is less than 25 MB in size. Unfortunately, Parliament's servers are not exactly cutting edge and struggle to cope with large files. However, unless you intend to send your hi-res holiday snaps along with your submission, the file size is unlikely to be a problem.

According to the official guidelines across the select committees, you should send a Microsoft Word document (in doc, docx, rtf, txt ooxml or odt format) rather than a PDF and should keep the use of large company logos or embedded pictures to a minimum (this is where you are likely to fall foul of breaching the file size requirements). The submission should also be one single document rather than a number of attachments which could get separated – this includes any annexes or appendices. I would always advise that the document is kept as simple as possible: plain text, perhaps a small logo and then a nicely laid out document of a few pages which is accessible and easy to read. Do not go lower than font size 11 and try to increase the spacing to 1.5.

GETTING WITNESSES TO APPEAR

Once the committee has resolved to proceed with an inquiry, it then needs to decide who the witnesses may be, which is not always a simple process.

The first stage is establishing the organisation or person

(if the inquiry is focused on the actions of an individual, although this is relatively rare) that is best placed to speak about the issues being examined. Committees are not usually that imaginative.

Let me give you an example to illustrate how this works. If there was to be an inquiry into the future of the high street, the committee would likely begin with big-name brands which feature in most major UK towns:

- Marks & Spencer – often seen as the bellwether company for retail issues.
- John Lewis – politically popular partly due to its employee-owned structure.
- Boots – seen as having a vital role in the community due to its pharmacy services.
- Costa Coffee – always seen positively compared with alleged tax-dodging rivals.
- Nando's – mid-market brand with a trendy clientele.

This would ensure the inquiry hearings are relevant to almost every parliamentary constituency in the UK. For example, at the time of writing, Boots has around 2,500 stores in the UK; Costa has 2,467; M&S has 1,035; John Lewis/Waitrose has 400; and Nando's has 392. This fact makes it more interesting to the media who monitor these events as anything surprising could then feature in the subsequent business coverage.

The committee would then think about who else would provide a valuable angle on the debate, or at least an association with the issue. It might include:

- a celebrity figure, as we saw in Part 2, such as retailer and TV star Mary Portas, who once led a government review of the high street;
- representatives of the major business groups, such as the British Chambers of Commerce or the British Retail Consortium;
- a high-profile former retail CEO, such as Sir Stuart Rose;
- an academic, to add intellectual weight to proceedings; or
- figures from local government who could share their experiences from specific councils of business rates and urban regeneration.

The list of other targets would primarily feature representatives from the government who would be required to give evidence as the inquiry draws to a close. This would feature the relevant minister alongside relevant civil servants at the Department for Business, Energy and Industrial Strategy.

Part of the reason for meeting with the 'expert witnesses' prior to the government's session is to get help in skewering the minister, official, company or individual. Committee officials must always think ahead and plot what each witness is likely to say, and how the totality of the oral evidence fits together. What committees really want is to get a range of organisations before them to identify significant policy failures and then unleash that information upon a minister, hoping that the pressure leads to a promise to review or immediately initiate a policy change. Being a minister often requires putting out small fires, so if they can throw an initiative or a small sum of cash at a problem, they can potentially neutralise it before it becomes more politically damaging.

Once the chosen organisations have been agreed by the committee's chair, the officials must pursue the relevant individuals within those organisations. The official guidance is: 'Where the witness is an organisation, it is usually left to the organisation to decide which of its members or staff should represent it at the hearing. Committees may, however, request the attendance of specific individuals or post holders.'[124]

This grey area makes the decision trickier. As a rule of thumb, a committee will always seek the most senior possible representative of a company to appear. In theory, that makes perfect sense; after all, the CEO would seem appropriate, given that they have the greatest say on a company's behaviour and actions. But there are other key reasons why the committee zeroes in on people at this level.

Firstly, there is ego; the committee (rightly) sees itself as a representative of the wider public's interests, and therefore believes that this warrants the time of the most senior individual in an organisation. But, secondly, the committee knows full well that the CEO has the most to lose in appearing. I have been in-house when a CEO has been called before a committee and panic often ensues, but not always for the reason you might imagine.

It is surprising how often the CEO is not the appropriate witness, simply because he or she does not always know enough about the issue under scrutiny within their own company. As one current select committee chair told me, 'CEOs are successful people at the top of their careers, but politics is a unique profession and you have got to understand our mindset before you go into the room to answer our questions.'

For this to be shown to the public at large in the event of the appearance going wrong would be incredibly embarrassing, and so often the aim is to find another less senior victim within the organisation.

The committee may not expect to always get their target man or woman, but they do not often admit that to the company invited to attend. At the very least, they would expect to be given an extremely compelling reason as to why the CEO cannot be present.

Let me give you an example of the approach some companies have taken successfully. If you have a tech firm such as Twitter, then a major policy issue which triggers a Digital, Culture, Media and Sport Committee inquiry into their behaviour is probably better fronted by a Twitter employee based in the UK who has day-to-day responsibility for that issue in this country (even though they may be a small fish in the global structure of the firm). Even the committee is privately likely to accept that the CEO of Twitter cannot have oversight of every single exchange which happens on a platform with around 326 million active worldwide users per month.

On even rarer occasions, companies have managed to extricate themselves entirely from a witness invitation with the committee's blessing, but the odds are against them doing so. A company may strike really lucky if the committee has such diary restraints that it can offer only one date for a specific witness to appear and the proposed witness has an

existing event in the diary which cannot be reasonably re-
scheduled – for example, the CEO of a multinational has an
AGM on that exact day, which was clearly set many months
in advance. Not even the cruellest committee chair would
force that individual to appear if it is clear that it would have
a detrimental impact on their business.

However, it gets harder where the issue does not necessarily require the CEO but could instead feature someone
else who is qualified to speak on behalf of the company.
This could be another member of the company's board, but
sometimes even a more junior policy specialist.

One method I have used with a client in the past was to write
down the positives and negatives about each of the two most
knowledgeable internal candidates to appear. In the instance
below, one was the CEO and the other was a senior head at
the business. I went into the process clear that the head was the
right person, and they ultimately agreed; nevertheless, this was
a very illuminating process in which we all challenged ourselves
to fairly explore the case for both. It looked something like this:
Pros for the CEO as witness:

- His reputation in the industry could be diminished by
  being seen to have 'run scared'.
- The committee is likely to ask 'Why did your CEO not
  agree to appear?', leading to some uncomfortable questions at the beginning of the session.
- He is a very adept communicator.
- He has an overall view of the business, not just the aspect
  being examined by the committee.

Cons for the CEO as witness:

- It is a reputational risk for the business to put forward the most senior leader.
- The committee's inquiry description focuses upon a specific strand of business activity; the CEO is not an expert in that area of activity.
- His manner may be too polished for an aggressive select committee.
- He would require extra training compared with the divisional head, which creates extra diary pressures.

As well as agreeing who the witness should be, it also led to an honest conversation within the business about some of its key strengths and weaknesses, which helped to clarify our thinking and enabled us to properly prepare.

Once the list of witnesses has been secured, the committee confirms the sequencing of who appears and when, both of which are published on the committee's website.

CAN YOU SAY NO?

I know what you are thinking. 'Maybe I can avoid having to appear at all, citing a busy diary or some other excuse?' My very strong advice is that this short-term tactic is a massive mistake and it is foolish to say no, not least because your longer-term reputation depends on you being seen to be a leader and not running away.

In the modern business era, the idea of shareholder primacy (the notion that the only responsibility that companies have is to their shareholders, rather than to worry about the communities in which they are located, their employees or the environment, for example) is under threat. Therefore, corporate leaders are expected to do more than just run a business. Instead, they are seen as 'thought leaders', trying to actively raise standards by acting ethically and transparently. If that is the case then how does it look for a CEO or other senior person within the business to decide that he or she does not wish to provide an explanation of a situation to Parliament and to the wider public?

Like it or lump it, if you are an organisation that proclaims to be actively engaged in wider society, as most do in their annual reports, then you should pretty much accept that you will need to appear and begin to prepare accordingly. That is the informal case for why you should just accept a select committee request to appear, but prodding the committee into making an example of you is just not sensible business behaviour, whatever the outcome.

TRAINING

OK, so now the committee has launched its inquiry, it has 'persuaded' you to attend to give oral evidence and you have a date to appear. From this point on it is all about training and preparing for the challenge ahead. The more time you invest, the easier it will be to deliver a successful outcome.

As I mentioned at the beginning of this section, some

people have natural talents which help to make them good at appearing before a select committee. Charisma is, it is generally agreed, not easy to teach. Experience cannot be taught at all, but comes as a result of involvement in an issue. But the other essential quality, eloquence, can definitely be harnessed through the right training.

Let me outline what makes a good witness, who can not only satisfy the demands of the various select committees, but also survive them:

- Being helpful – the good witness is seen to go with the grain of the select committee hearing, not seeking to obfuscate, over-spin or deceive. This does not mean giving the committee everything it wants (that would make you a bad witness!), but is more a case of giving them enough to be seen as having added to the pool of knowledge.

- Being informative – for all the grandstanding they often deploy, select committees are ultimately there to generate and clarify information which adds to an awareness of any given issue. Whether you are under fire or providing the expert witness, your role is to deploy your knowledge. If you can make the committee look wiser for having received your input, then all the better for everyone.

- Being deferential – you may detest politicians and you may believe that the inquiry hearing is being conducted for all the wrong reasons, but you should certainly not make that obvious. In fact, you should do the opposite. Yes, it is important to stand up for yourself where you believe false or inaccurate claims have been levied against you, but you must not forget the fact that the committee represents a vital function in our parliamentary democracy, and the MPs are all elected. In short, leave any bitter resentment at the entrance to Parliament and engage with the process.

- Being courteous – added to the deferential nature of your appearance, you should also remain polite at all times, ensuring that however bad things get, you are seen to have behaved appropriately throughout. You can be a strong witness on the policy issues, but if you are seen to have behaved arrogantly then you will have undone all your good work.

In contrast, here is an outline of what constitutes a bad appearance:

- Being aggressive – so often we see witnesses appear who make it abundantly clear that they do not respect the process and cannot help but get the tone all wrong. The classic example of this was Philip Green, the chair of Arcadia Group, who made an infamous solo appearance before the joint Work and Pensions and Business Committees, as described in Part 1. The more irritable he got with the committee, the longer they kept him there. It really was self-defeating behaviour from Green, if the aim was to get out of the room as soon as possible.

- Being argumentative – there is a big difference between

standing up for yourself by making your position clear to a committee and being belligerent. The latter will ultimately irritate the MPs or peers asking you questions and could lead to unnecessary friction.

- Being weak on detail – in some ways, this is the worst mistake of all. Committees may not react well to poor personal behaviour but if the committee ultimately concludes that taking your evidence has been a complete waste of their time then the reputational damage to you and your organisation is maximised. The classic example of this was Andrew Cecil, who represented Amazon at the infamous Public Accounts Committee hearing into aggressive tax practices. As described in Part 1, Cecil did not appear to understand his own business, constantly needing to apologise to the committee for not having information to hand and promising to follow up with a letter at a later date. As Margaret Hodge finally concluded, 'Mr Cecil, you don't have anything! Honestly, you have come to us with absolutely no information. What is your job?'

- Being unprepared – this is less about being weak on detail but more about the appearance itself, and the reason why training is so important. A witness who just pitches up to a hearing and seemingly has not considered what information is required to assist the committee is not going to emerge with their reputation intact. It is entirely avoidable and not forgivable in the eyes of parliamentarians.

There is a myth that you need to eradicate from your mind as soon as possible after you have been called or compelled to appear. I have lost count of the number of times that clients have suggested to me that a select committee hearing represents an 'opportunity' for them to get their views across and win the argument. To paraphrase Margaret Thatcher, no, no, no, no and no again. While I admire the confidence and optimism they are projecting with this statement, they are invariably wrong. As one committee chair told me, 'Some of my biggest hits have come by accident due to a witness who unwisely doesn't shut up.'

I have two football analogies to illustrate this point. Firstly, as with a football referee, the best witnesses are those you do not even notice. When a football match becomes focused on the performance of the referees, then something controversial or unsavoury has happened. It is the same with select committee witnesses – you want to leave that committee session with no likelihood of a recall and no one talking about you.

You must also ensure that you minimise the number of questions you will be asked. Just like a football team that is 1–0 ahead against a tough opponent, you should try to take the ball into the corner, waste time and hope you can just keep your opponents at bay.

You should keep in mind the actual powers of the select committee. It will either be a direct shadow of the specific department or have a cross-departmental focus. Either way, the committee can only ever suggest policy change to government ministers or suggest that a company boss should resign or pay back a bonus. On that basis, what should your strategy be? The starting point is always to survive. As we have already seen in this book, the chairs of the committees, both past and present, intend the experience to be gruelling. The witness's wish to shine is not shared by the committee.

Am I being cynical? Well, perhaps – but that is because the process is largely cynical and I am just being realistic. As a witness, you are a fox to be devoured by the pack of hounds, like *Love Island* contestants are to the tabloids.

My advice, therefore, is to always go into your evidence session minus any fear or loathing of the people who are asking the questions. They do, after all, represent the views of around 75,000 constituents in their locality, and they are part of the democratic legislative chamber. They do have the right to ask you questions on policy – but they do not have the right to force you into a poor performance. Only you can do that by not preparing or training sufficiently. It may seem a slightly odd technique (well, yes it is), but when you are fielding questions, imagine they are being asked by all of the people each MP represents. If that many people in a room were demanding answers, you would certainly sit up straight and answer with great care. This technique helps you to mentally ignore the pomposity of the individual MP and helps you to keep in mind the validity of the process.

You should begin your research and training by identifying one of the key elements of your appearance: to be in total command of the facts. The first thing is to be honest with yourself and/or your organisation. It is best to just start with a meeting in which there is total honesty and you get all the facts out on the table, regardless of how uncomfortable they may be. This is one thing you can usually control. Whether you share all those facts is another matter, but you need to know what happened within your own organisation and why.

I had one particularly significant client who appeared before a select committee where the three individuals had been participants in a project which had ultimately ended in failure and a major corporate collapse. Although they were colleagues, they had often worked separately during the period in which they were advising the company in question.

Had there not been a select committee hearing, it is unlikely the three people would have got together to pick over the bones of the dreadful outcome of their project work – at least, not in the short term. Being called to give evidence changed all that, and the process forced them to sit in a room together and start trying to better understand what exactly had gone wrong. The initial meeting was very tricky and very bumpy, but it allowed them to identify their various strengths and weaknesses in terms of the roles they had played. After the select committee had been successfully navigated, the three individuals reflected on that first meeting, and agreed that although it led to some harsh truths having to be faced (even more challenging given there were a bunch of external people in the room listening), it ultimately ensured that the committee could not divide them and take a free hit. The ultimate appearance was co-ordinated and seamless as a result.

This need for clarity should also drive the decision as to who will be the representative for your organisation, in the event that you are actually given a choice. As we have already identified, the committee will go extremely hard on any witness who does not appear to have sufficient detail. If it is a CEO, this can be even more damaging, especially when given the classic reply to a perceived non-answer from the witness: 'Either you are lying, or you are clueless.' The more your arguments can be substantiated by figures, facts and examples, the better. It becomes harder for the committee to make a case against you if their assertions have been (politely) batted back with an impressive display of detail and knowledge.

On this basis, a good first move is to take a sheet of paper and list every strength and weakness associated with your personal actions, and/or those of your company. Let me demonstrate what this might look like, using an example of a bank whose customers suffered a data breach.

Positives (individual/company):

- As soon as I was informed about the incident, I launched our internal contingency plan and convened a conference call of my senior team.
- I gave instructions for a customer communications bulletin to be sent within twelve hours of the incident being reported.
- I have requested an independent investigation into what went wrong and its causes.

Negatives (individual/company):

- I have since discovered that we had been warned that our systems may not be sufficiently protected from a major hack of this kind and we did not act upon that advice.
- Although I did get our contingency planning into action

when I was told, there was a delay of several hours prior to my being informed.

- We did not communicate to customers in the first twelve hours, nor to the wider media, which led to increased panic.
- No one internally has been disciplined or has lost their job.
- My remuneration committee has recently approved a significant increase in my next bonus and it will not look good.

This exercise allows you to map out where the major challenges lie in advance of the select committee hearing and helps you to focus on the key issues where you feel exposed. This will also give you the opportunity to better develop a Q&A and key messages document, which is where you will hone your skills prior to appearing.

Developing a Q&A is standard practice in communications preparation because it is about anticipating difficult questions which may be asked by the media or political audiences. It is especially important in preparing for a select committee.

My usual advice is to have two Q&As – one which covers every eventuality you think could come up (including questions which may seem a bit left-field but could catch you out), as well as a more focused one. The latter will be easier for the witness themselves to use in preparation, and is often prepared as a 'top ten toughest questions'. In reality, if someone is considered senior enough to represent the company in such a high-profile forum, then we have to assume they know enough about the operating performance of the business to be able to answer most questions. If they don't, then surely they should not be appearing in the first place. However, the 'top ten' focus means they can be prepared for the questions where there is currently no satisfactory answer.

Following on from a completed Q&A document, you need to work on honing your messaging, which means succinct ways of explaining your position, and/or that of your organisation, on any given issue. It is ultimately about finding eloquent ways to explain yourself. You may well have the facts in your head, but not everyone is a natural communicator. Message development is likely to highlight key themes and provide a succinct one- or two-paragraph message that the witness can learn by rote, or at least of which they have an understanding and can tailor on the day.

I am going to give you a real example of a client who appeared before the Housing, Communities and Local Government Committee, to give you a sense of what ideal preparation looks like. This major company, which is a familiar high street restaurant chain, was notified on 3 November that they would be appearing on 3 December. This, fortunately, provided plenty of prior notice in order to prepare.

We then broke down the process as follows:

- 5 November: Conference call to discuss details of the select committee inquiry, identify the risks and the right witness and to agree on the training needs of that person.

- 9 November: Created and sent to the witness an information pack about the specific committee, such as biographies, photos, dos and don'ts and a summary of the evidence the committee had already taken.

- 16 November: First training meeting with the witness. This was a two-hour meeting where the information pack was brought to life. The conversation identified the data which the witness felt they lacked from the business, and the initial set of likely questions were talked through.

- 18 November: The first set of draft answers for the likely questions were produced and sent to the witness to absorb and begin to reimagine in their own voice and natural style.

- 20 November: Key people within the business replied with the facts designed to answer the likely questions.

- 23 November: This was an informal dress rehearsal of the questioning, but with the witness having the opportunity to pause, reflect and start again on an answer. This was an exercise to get the brain working and to get warmed up for the most testing and challenging practice to come the following week. Key messages were also developed, as a means of being able to provide a general principle to any question.

- 27 November: Full-scale dress rehearsal which had no breaks whatsoever and played out the select committee hearing as though it were for real – testing, prodding, annoying and interrupting. This mock hearing lasted exactly one hour, the expected duration of the actual committee hearing. After a brief break for refreshments, the group then sat down and reviewed what was good and what could be improved.

- 30 November: This was a one-to-one session with me and the witness. I posed some of the key questions in an aggressive style but focused on the top five most difficult questions and issues. Like an exam, there was no real time for cramming answers now; it was a case of staying mentally sharp and fresh.

- 3 December: The appearance itself.

I am pleased to say that the hearing was a great success, and the preparation ensured that there was not a question that my witness could not answer. The body language was great, the answers pithy and interesting, yet not too much so.

The programme of training that I have outlined was structured for that specific time frame, but you will not always have the luxury of a month's notice. You could be required to appear in a week, or even a matter of days. In that instance, the training programme would need to be tailored accordingly.

DRESS REHEARSALS

Using dress rehearsals as a means of preparing for a committee hearing is often the most important aspect of your preparation. It is relatively easy to be asked a question, have the time and space to play about with the answer and then discuss how best to respond with a team of advisors in a room. It is another challenge entirely to be repeatedly hit with aggressive questions in real time, and have to think on your feet under extreme pressure. This is usually why most select committee hearings go wrong.

You may initially consider it to be demeaning to receive full training prior to a hearing. After all, you run a major business and carry out a wide range of public engagements in your day job and experience few problems. But it is often this arrogance that could be your undoing. If you believe that you know everything, then you probably do not.

Question training is best split into two separate sessions. The first one is designed to start asking questions which could emerge in the course of the hearing, but without making it a real-time interrogation. This allows tough questions to be asked but gives you the breathing space to answer and practise the options available. If a question poses a real challenge, it can then be discussed and you can figure out what you need in terms of further research to answer it. Throughout the process of an inquiry, the committee will be actively thinking about the subsequent report it will need to publish, so will be looking for clear recommendations they can make when it is completed. Although typically the report reflects the prejudices the committee holds prior to the start of the inquiry, you can sometimes help to reshape some of the conclusions by the strength of your oral evidence; therefore, the more tools that you can give them to find in your favour, the better. In the absence of data, the committee will be more reliant on baseless assertions.

The full dress rehearsal is about taking the preparation to the highest level. The whole purpose of this session is to test all the systems fully and exert maximum pressure. Ideally, you need to take the dress rehearsal away from your office or home and into a location with which you are not familiar.

Wherever the training location is, make sure that the room is set up in a style which is similar to how it will look in Parliament. That means a confrontational seating plan, where the questioners effectively surround the witness in a semicircle. There should be no real discussion beforehand, and having strangers also attend and ask questions is another good idea, to emphasise the environment you will have to deal with on the day.

Have a session of at least forty-five minutes to an hour, and make the questions as tough as possible. Do have people who interrupt, challenge, nitpick, annoy and generally play to the cameras. On the latter point, I often film the training sessions so that you can see for yourself how you come across on screen. It can sometimes help you when you are being advised on body language or your tone of voice. If a witness is ever going to lose patience or lose their temper, then a dress rehearsal is the place to do it, rather than in the actual hearing itself.

After the final training session, it is good for the people training you to provide feedback around the room, but with a few caveats. This is not the moment for them to reveal problems that can't really be fixed – for example, picking on a personal weakness – as this will only cause worry or distress in advance of the appearance. You should seek feedback which is constructive and which you can process in the forthcoming day or two. It is also a good idea for your trainers to agree beforehand a spokesperson to summarise all the feedback, rather than twenty people all having their say.

Just remember that doing this exercise is hard, and retaining all the facts and correcting any body language issues you may have is not easy. Do not make yourself miserable and anxious before the big day. There comes a point, as with exam revision, when the brain struggles to take anything more on board and trying to soak up more information becomes self-defeating. At this stage, the best thing you can do is get a good night's sleep.

USE LAWYERS CAREFULLY

I have to admit that there is often a historical tension between communications advisors and lawyers when it comes to preparing witnesses for select committees.

This is because of a fundamental difference in the type of advice we provide. Communications advisors are often focused on finding ways to tell a story as effectively as possible. Sometimes this involves defending a position but other times it may mean simply apologising for wrongdoing. It is the latter that sometimes upsets the lawyers.

From their perspective, they are seeking to defend a client in every way possible even if there is reputational damage sustained along the way. Taking an extreme example, O. J. Simpson's lawyers were focused only on keeping their client out of jail – they did not have time to fret over the long-term reputational consequences for him. This means that they will often advise witnesses not to answer certain questions and to provide as scant information as possible, as well as ensuring key messages are carefully scrutinised, signed off and agreed in advance, in a way which goes beyond what communications advisors would require.

The other danger of external lawyers being heavily involved in the preparation for a select committee is that the size of the Q&A and other briefing documents becomes completely unwieldy. Not to be cynical (god forbid), but most legal firms charge by the hour, which undoubtedly incentivises them to extend their work – hence, a twenty-page Q&A document could easily become five times that size if legal advisors take over the process.

This is not a rant about lawyers' lack of understanding of politics, but they do sometimes miss the point of what the select committees represent and misunderstand the mindset of members on them. It is on this basis that I would advise being careful about how you use legal advisors when preparing for a select committee hearing.

Before I ruin my relationship with the legal profession (with whom I frequently work!), I do not mean to say that it is a waste of time, as lawyers can offer a very valuable additional view. Just make sure you use them sparingly, and do not rely on them solely for advice in a political arena; it is best to use them in conjunction with the type of advice my industry offers.

Nevertheless, here is a real-life example of a case on which I worked where the lawyers got their way, and probably rightly.

Back in 2015, it came to light that a car manufacturer had introduced a software update which had affected the emissions output of a car when being tested for pollution levels in a laboratory. In the United States, this caused a very serious problem indeed, with criminal investigations and a major consumer outcry. The software became known as a 'defeat device', allegedly designed to cheat the test system and allow the company to suppress emission levels when in test conditions in order to meet strict regulatory standards.

The primary focus of the company was on managing the problem in its two biggest markets, Germany and the United States; the third biggest market was the United Kingdom. However, in Europe the regulations are written in a slightly different way so that the definition of a 'defeat device' was not the same as in the US.

In the United States, the company did what it needed to do to escape further censure. It unreservedly apologised for what had happened, suspended the technicians who had been involved in the incident and paid around $18 billion in compensation.

However, because the European regulations differed, the company was not in breach of them, and therefore it became clear that compensation may not be payable. The local solution was to offer free software fixes to the customer and provide some other discounts.

For the UK select committees, this response was unacceptable. In their eyes, the company had cheated and should be held to account in the same way as they had been in the United States. Unsurprisingly, the company started getting requests to appear before the committees – initially the Transport Committee (twice), the Environmental Audit Committee, and the Environment, Food and Rural Affairs Committee. Four separate inquiry sessions is a very unusual and no doubt punishing experience for the business head for the UK, who went before all of them.

For this individual, it became a difficult matter in terms of what they could say regarding the issue in Europe. Communications advisors such as me would say that in this situation, you apologise for what has happened, explain what you're doing to put it right and then unveil a package of compensation measures to alleviate the problem.

The legal position, however, highlighted that accepting blame, or at least agreeing that the software download was a 'defeat device', would open the company up to litigation across EU member states, which could result in liabilities as high as those in the United States. Taking a position to admit wrongdoing could have been very costly and may have led to serious implications for the senior executives involved, perhaps even prison.

On that basis, the lawyers won and quite rightly, even though the four sessions were bruising and mentally draining. In the end, the committees ranted and raved about the company and perceived bad behaviour, but that was as far as it went. The company was not classed as having broken the law in the UK or elsewhere in Europe.

COLLUSION

'Collusion' may be too strong a word, but is it ever acceptable for multiple witnesses on a panel to discuss their hearing in advance? In theory, the committee would frown on this activity and, if they knew about it, could make an example of you in the hearing. But unless you are very foolish and tell them, then some form of discussion is obviously sensible and can be helpful. However, there are of course various factors to consider. Firstly, can you trust the other witness when they say they will have your back during the session? You need to have a few daggers ready just in case you come under attack. Secondly, will it be too obvious that you have colluded by the stilting and over-practised response you might give? Lastly, who benefits most from the attempted collusion? If it's genuinely a 50/50 mutual benefit, then great – but, in reality, someone is likely to be better off and you should try to ensure it is you.

THE MEDIA

One thing it is very unwise to do is to brief the media in advance of your select committee appearance. This really upsets committee chairs and is a very risky approach. I recall a select committee on aviation where a communications representative from a budget airline tried to be far too clever and briefed the *Evening Standard* in advance to attack one of the other witnesses. He thought this would help to shape the debate and put his company into prime position. In reality, it had been spotted by the formidable chair of the Transport Committee, the late, great Labour MP Gwyneth Dunwoody, and she began the session with an excruciating attack on the budget airline and warned him that it would be noted by the committee and any such behaviour in future would be punished. Needless to say, he did not do it again. Here is the exchange:

> Chair: Gentlemen, I am afraid I have an unpleasant duty to perform. The *Evening Standard* today has come out with an article which frankly causes us very great

concern. People who give the evidence they intend to give to a Select Committee to another party, and particularly to anyone in the Press, before they arrive are actually committing contempt of the House of Commons. The reason why you are asked to come here and give evidence and the reason why we decide what we will do with that evidence is that it is a duty of those who appear here to understand that we are a Select Committee and the House of Commons examines that evidence. I must say to those who are quoted, in this case Mr Nicol, it says: 'Speaking ahead of his appearance before the Committee today, easyJet Director said there is a case for urgent reform,' and then there is a long quote from you. This is, frankly, not acceptable. In the worst possible cases, we then have to decide whether or not we intend to take evidence from you. We have, however, discussed this. We are extraordinarily unhappy. Have you any comment you wish to make?

Toby Nicol: No. Thank you very much for pointing that out and thank you if you continue to take evidence from me, and apologies.

Chair: Did I hear a particular word?

Toby Nicol: Apologies.

Chair: Good.

Any interaction with journalists is thus best handled by waiting until after the session has ended. When in doubt, play it safe.

ON THE DAY

TAKE CARE OF YOURSELF

Now that all the preparation has been done and dusted, you should be feeling a greater sense of confidence, even if naturally still a little anxious about the big day. It is vitally important to get sufficient rest for the following day's activities. Without a good night's sleep, you will have reduced cognitive function, and you will struggle to maintain focus and an even temper.

You must also allow yourself some time to absorb and reflect on what you have learned over the previous few days or weeks.

On the day itself, depending on the time your session starts, avoid a journey which potentially puts you under pressure and fighting against the clock. As we all know, British transport is hardly the most reliable and this would be a really bad time for it to let you down. There was one particular instance where a sudden snowfall left a witness I had been training stranded in the countryside. Fortunately, they made it just in time, but the unnecessary stress was not the ideal preparation and it took them a while to settle down and get into a flow during the evidence session.

For some of us, it will be beyond our means, but if you are representing a large company with an expense account it is worth considering staying overnight in London prior to your appearance. This cuts out many of the potential calamities you might encounter if you hop on the train, bus or motorway.

As well as a good sleep and a stress-free journey, eating the right things in advance of your session is also important. I would suggest a light breakfast if it is early, and it is arguably even more important to eat properly should the hearing take place in the afternoon. The challenging thing about a mid-to-late afternoon select committee hearing is that you have been forced to fret and worry all day long, and thereby tire yourself out by the time you sit down before the committee.

Either way, eat light, definitely do not drink alcohol in advance (although feel free to get well refreshed in the pub afterwards, of course). The key is to eat food which will provide energy in the morning, and a light lunch in the afternoon, as well as to make sure you stay well hydrated (not least given that sometimes the witnesses cannot even get a drink of water during the hearing itself). You may choose to boost yourself with a coffee to stay alert, but not too much if caffeine makes you anxious. You may assume that the sheer adrenalin rush of being before the cameras will shock your system into action throughout, and that is broadly true, but over the course of a long session you will undoubtedly begin to flag.

Some foods you might consider for breakfast, prior to a morning select committee hearing include eggs (especially boiled, poached or scrambled) and sources of slow release energy such as porridge, unsweetened yogurt and fresh fruit.

At lunchtime, you might try a light lunch that is high in protein, such as tuna or grilled chicken, accompanied by brown rice or potatoes.

Whether they are packed with carbs for readily available energy, or fibre and protein for a slower release of energy, these foods can help increase your power and stamina as you face the challenges ahead.

The food types to avoid include anything high in sugar which will give you a quick boost but will crash you during your evidence session; fatty foods which are likely to make you sleepy and sluggish; and anything too spicy as you do not want to irritate your already nervous stomach.

The former Conservative leader William Hague said that eating properly was his first piece of advice to David Cameron when he became Leader of the Opposition. There is no reason why you should not follow suit.

When I am training more than one person for a high-profile session, I usually meet with the witnesses for what I call a 'chemistry' meeting, so they can chat informally to warm up for the final preparations and get mentally prepared for the hearing appearance. We then physically take the witness(es) to the select committee room ourselves, to act as logistical support. This is obviously a role that can be taken on by your own people if they have the requisite knowledge.

Whether the appearance is in the morning or the afternoon, I always recommend securing a venue near to Parliament from which to base yourself and any advisors that you are using for support. The options nearby are surprisingly poor, but there are definitely some good venues to consider, such as these four which I have used in the past:

- Institute for Civil Engineers (ICE). Address: 1 Great George Street, Westminster, London SW1P 3AA. It is a five-minute walk from Parliament Square to either Portcullis House or St Stephen's entrance of the main Parliament building. This venue, just off Parliament Square has discreet meeting rooms and offers food and refreshments.

- Conrad London St James Hotel. Address: 22–28 Broadway, Westminster, London SW1H 0BH. This is a high-end option, and just an eight-minute walk to Parliament.

- Park Plaza Westminster Bridge London Hotel. Address: 200 Westminster Bridge Road, Lambeth, London SE1 7UT. This is a brisk eleven-minute walk if you want to get the blood flowing and some air in your lungs to steady the nerves.

- DoubleTree by Hilton Hotel. Address: 30 John Islip Street, Westminster, London SW1P 4DD. This is also an eleven-minute walk away, but has great facilities.

Of course, there is a cost implication with all of these options, but for a major company it is surely a worthwhile investment to get the preparation right. At the time of writing, you are likely to need to budget for £300–£600 to get a private room, food and other facilities, such as a projector screen for a laptop.

WHAT TO WEAR

Admittedly, this may not be at the forefront of your mind when it comes to the gruelling experience of appearing before a select committee, but it should not be dismissed out of hand. What you wear can be very important.

I bet, like me, you have watched the news and wondered aloud why a presenter chose to wear a particularly mismatched outfit or a hideous tie which was clearly a Christmas gift from a distant relative. It can be so off-putting that what the person is saying is lost. In your appearance before the committee, it makes sense to minimise the distraction your sartorial choices may cause. Beyond the need to show respect to the committee, you don't want to look scruffy on camera, given friends and family are also watching!

What to wear in Parliament has been a source of great anguish over the years, even for MPs. In 1900, a new set of rules had to be written to clarify the etiquette regarding tall hats, which had become fashionable. The author, Alfred Kinnear MP, wrote:

At all times remove your hat on entering the House, and put it on upon taking your seat and remove it again on rising for whatever purpose. If the MP asks a question he will stand, and with his hat off; and he may receive the answer of the Minister seated and with his hat on.

You may be puzzled and amazed to learn that MPs were, until the late 1990s, able to wear a large, black top hat (often dubbed an 'opera hat') to draw attention to themselves with the Speaker of the House of Commons. They were scrapped by the select committee on Commons Modernisation because they made the House 'look ridiculous'.[125]

On the basis that you do not intend to wear a top hat on your own appearance before a committee, for men, it is very easy. Just keep it nice and simple – boring, even. Always dress smartly, even if you work for a cutting-edge tech firm, because you need to show respect to the committee. That means a plain white or blue shirt, a dark grey or navy suit and a tie. You would not go to court wearing casual clothing, and the same applies to a committee.

For women, it is admittedly more difficult as there is greater freedom to get it wrong, but again the advice is to keep it simple. Smart business attire is always the default option, especially if you are being grilled for alleged wrongdoing. Boring always works in this instance.

ROOM LAYOUT

The layout of the select committee room will depend on where in the parliamentary estate you will be appearing.

If the committee is meeting in the Palace of Westminster, you will enter through Cromwell Green entrance, opposite Westminster Abbey, and identify yourself as a select committee witness to one of the visitor assistants (who can be identified by their distinctive dark blue uniform which has a portcullis on the front).

If the committee is meeting in Portcullis House (PCH), enter the building from the Victoria Embankment. In an ideal world, this is where you will get to appear. This building was opened in 2001 amidst some controversy about spiralling costs and rented trees (don't ask), but it has the big advantage of being purpose-built and modern unlike the Victorian conditions of its more famous cousin.

The rooms in PCH are much improved, with good lighting, plenty of space and fantastic acoustics. The latter is especially important, because if you are struggling to hear the questions being asked, then it immediately puts you under more pressure and could affect your performance.

In the older part of the parliamentary estate, the committee rooms are on an upstairs corridor. The carpet beneath your feet will either be green or red, reflecting whether you are in the part belonging to the Commons or the Lords. These rooms are very impressive in their own way, with flock wallpaper and wooden panelling; it is genuinely like being back in the Victorian era. However, these rooms are far from an ideal place to give evidence. They get extremely hot in summer, but are often overheated during winter too. The TV cameras in these rooms manage to make almost everyone look shifty. They also cram in the watching public right behind the witnesses, which can add to the effect of a person being on trial.

In both instances, witnesses usually have to wait outside the room before being allowed in to give their evidence. This can be slightly challenging too, as members of the public and journalists can freely mingle. For this reason, many high-profile witnesses will come straight up from entering the building into the committee room, ushered by committee assistants.

It is unlikely that the person who is being trained is a regular visitor to either Portcullis House or the main committee corridor of the Commons. This unfamiliarity could be distracting, and you want to eliminate every possible factor that could alter performance.

Therefore, if you have an advisor you may want them to take you to the site of the select committee hearing in advance just so you can get familiar with the surroundings. This can be done quite easily because, as a member of the public, you are permitted to watch a select committee hearing in either the newer or the older part of the parliamentary estate.

THE COMMITTEE PRE-MEET

Prior to a session getting underway, the committees meet briefly in private to discuss what questions to ask and what issues to focus on at the public meeting when the witness is present. While you would hope that the MPs are not just beginning to think about how the session will proceed at this late stage, sadly this is often the case; an MP I used to work with usually looked at his briefing papers for the first time as he entered the committee room. Once the pre-meeting has concluded, the witnesses, media and public are then invited in to take their seats. Members will ask questions and follow up on witnesses' responses.

Members may then meet in private to discuss what they have heard, although this is less common than the pre-meet. As the process develops, committees also meet in private to consider the conduct of their inquiries, to review their emerging conclusions and to consider their reports and recommendations.

GOING IN EARLY

Upon arrival, you will need to explain to security that you are a select committee witness and, if necessary, you can ask to be escorted straight to the committee room. This is helpful given that, at various points of the day, the queues outside Portcullis House and St Stephen's entrance can be huge. (These often horrendous queues, incidentally, have never been the subject of a parliamentary committee!) At the very least, the security officers will point you in the right direction. The committee's clerk will also be anxious to ensure that you get to the right room on time, so you will have plenty of people willing to help you through the various scanners and up the stairs swiftly. Being late is a cardinal sin for anyone appearing before a select committee, so plan your time as carefully as possible. Let's be honest, it is always going to be the biggest thing on that particular day in your diary, so clear the rest of it. The latest you should arrive at Westminster is twenty minutes before you are due to appear before the committee.

Unless you are the first witness, it is likely that there will be other inquiry sessions on the day prior to your own. The decision as to whether you should attend those sessions is a tricky one, so forgive me for oscillating between two different points of view.

Committees usually want you to attend earlier and listen to the previous witnesses' evidence so that you are in a position to comment on that evidence. Personally, I don't favour this approach. My usual advice is that you should not sit in on the previous session in person, especially if you or your company is the focus of the inquiry. If that is the case, then it is possible that cameras and journalists will intrude on you as you enter the building and room, and you'll be strained by the time you give evidence.

Sitting for over an hour hearing your company being criticised or blamed can be troubling, not least because you have no right to respond during someone else's oral sessions. It also fills your head with new information, so you may tire mentally. Ultimately, you should try to avoid feeling angry or unnecessarily anxious, which is often a result of having others distract you from your key objective of remaining calm and composed. Plus, if you do not attend the earlier sessions, the committee are forced to repeat the information provided by the previous witnesses, thus burning up additional time.

Nevertheless, there are exceptions. If you are not the main focus of a potential kicking from the committee, and especially if it is your first time giving evidence, getting into the room beforehand does allow you to acclimatise and start to understand the direction of the questions.

There is also a compromise option. In the past, I have sometimes asked committee clerks to arrange a private room in Parliament in which the preceding evidence session can be viewed. This can be invaluable if you do not want to go straight into the room and listen for hours prior to your own hearing. This will be an opportunity to discuss any final questions and lines to take amongst your support team. Admittedly, the committee does not like to have to do this, and will doubtless be annoyed that I have even included it in this book – but there is no harm in asking. It primarily works where the hearing is very high profile.

The downside is that the level of organisation is not often great. There was one occasion when the committee's session was being screened correctly in our appointed room, yet there was no sound feed. We then switched to a laptop to watch via ParliamentLive, but the poor Wi-Fi coverage in the Palace of Westminster meant that the streaming quality was intermittent at best. Oh, and there was not a drop of water to be found. But it can be done successfully with proper planning.

When you arrive at the committee room, you will now be in the hands of the clerk, who will give you clear instructions as to what to do next. You will likely be asked to enter and take a seat at the witness table. The committee staff will normally put name cards at the table, so it will be clear where you are supposed to sit. The traditional set-up is to have the main witness, e.g. the CEO, in the middle with supporting witnesses either side.

SUPPORT MATERIALS

You can bring notes to a select committee to have in front of you, but play this very, very carefully and keep your supporting materials to a minimum. Having the materials on the table can sometimes ensure you do not need them at all. It is when you find yourself panicking in a moment where your mind has gone blank that mistakes can happen. At least you will know that you have the relevant facts to hand should you need them.

For obvious reasons, though, committees can get irked if the witness looks too well prepared. They know themselves, especially if they have previously served in a ministerial role, that a witness with a deep folder of carefully prepared facts and figures has had professional support. In a few instances over the years, the committee chairs have even gone as far as requesting the witness to hand over the folders to be shared with the committee. This would be very embarrassing, so I advise that you keep it to a bare minimum set of key facts over one to two pages, so if anyone looked at them, it would be considered harmless.

You also need to think about where your supporting team sits in the room. Quite often it can seem sensible to have your key advisors right behind you on the front row, but those people need to be very disciplined to ensure that: a) they do not pull faces, get visibly annoyed, shake their head, or make any number of other careless errors, and b) they do not pass you anything or speak to you during the session. MPs can get really angry when a witness's supporter is seen to be whispering advice into their ear. It may raise the question: who is really answering the committee's questions? If it is not the witness themselves, perhaps the committee should call the other person to appear too.

Before the questions begin, the members will usually be asked to declare any conflict of interest which could be relevant to the hearing. For example, the Labour MP Graham Stringer would always declare, when grilling the bosses at Heathrow, that he was a former chair of Manchester Airport and a member of Unite (a trade union which covers most airport baggage handlers). If the conflict of interest was too high, the member would be excused from being involved in a particular inquiry.

In the same way, you will be asked to provide your name, job title and company as a means of introduction, although sometimes the committee chair will do this directly. Either way, it is a means of identifying the witnesses for the official record of proceedings.

HOW TO CONDUCT YOURSELF

The manner in which you conduct yourself when you appear before a select committee is absolutely crucial in determining whether it will be a success or a failure.

Whatever your view of parliamentarians, you must enter the room utterly convinced of their right to ask whatever questions they wish. This isn't just a matter of respect for the important role that our elected Parliament plays in our democracy; it is about getting yourself into the right frame of mind to survive.

If you have complete and total disdain for the people asking you questions, your answers will reflect this and you could put yourself into a difficult position and risk reputational damage. This damage is, of course, a problem for the company or organisation you represent, but is also about you personally. At some point, you may move jobs and you carry your reputation with you wherever you go. If nothing else persuades you to take this preparation process seriously, that thought certainly should.

BODY LANGUAGE

Although you have to focus on the politicians in the committee room – ensuring good eye contact, for example – it is also the case that you need to be very mindful of the cameras which film parliamentary hearings. Image is everything and shifty body language, such as the way you hold your hands, and your tone of voice, can all be factors in how people perceive you.

Your body language is incredibly important. Make sure you sit upright and appear engaged even when not answering questions (particularly as the session is televised live). Viewers will often judge whether a witness is being open and transparent on the basis of how they sit, where they put their hands, if they shake their head or are seen to smirk.

It goes without saying that giving oral evidence to Parliament is generally a public process. The cameras are on, your words are transcribed and representatives of the media may be in the room if it is a really high-profile session.

A great deal of this people-watching element is figuring out whether the witness is telling the truth based on how they say it. Even the chairs themselves admit that they keenly study their witnesses for physical signs of lying. One former chair told me, 'I could always tell the guilty witness in a group of three or more, because they would be the quietest one and look to hide away!'

There are many ways that people reveal if they are telling the truth, most of which are not related to what they actually say, but to their actions.

According to fascinating insights from an ex-CIA agent, there are six tell-tale signs specialists look for to see if someone is lying. Even without their expert training, we naturally pick up on many of them. Select committee chairs are probably more adept than most because they are actively looking for signs that you are misleading the committee. The six signs the CIA looks for are:

- Behavioural pause or delay – this is where you ask a person a question and you initially get nothing in response. That is perfectly understandable if the question is 'What was the exact date you joined company X?', as this will require anyone to think hard to recall the information. However, if the question is 'Did you instruct your Finance Director to shred the documents before the police arrived?' then any pause seems rather incriminating.

- Verbal/non-verbal disconnect – this is where someone's head is gently moving side to side when they are verbalising a yes response, or vice versa. This can indicate that the person is saying something that they physically cannot prevent demonstrating to be false.

- Hiding the mouth or eyes – according to the CIA's experts, a deceptive person will often hide his or her mouth or eyes when being untruthful. There is a natural tendency to want to cover over a lie, so it is significant if a person's hand goes in front of their mouth while they are responding to a question. Similarly, there's a natural inclination to shield oneself from the reaction of those who are being lied to. If a person shields their eyes while they are responding to a question, they might well be indicating on a subconscious level that they cannot bear to see the reaction to the lie they are telling.

- Throat-clearing or swallowing – physiologically, the question might have created a spike in anxiety, which can cause discomfort or dryness in the mouth and throat.

- Hand-to-face activity – if a person is biting or licking their lips or pulling on their ears, it may indicate anxiety. A tough question may create a reaction because a truthful response would be incriminating. The nervous system then works to dissipate the anxiety, draining blood from the surfaces of the face, the ears and the extremities, which can create a sensation of cold or itchiness. The hands are then drawn to those areas to mitigate those physical feelings, providing another signal to those watching.

- Grooming gestures – a deceptive person will often fiddle with their tie or shirt cuffs, play with their jewellery or adjust their glasses. They might also run their fingers through their hair, or straighten their skirt. Tidying up the area around them is another form of grooming gesture. For example, a difficult question might trigger the individual to shuffle the papers in front of them, move the glass of water closer, or straighten the positioning of a pencil or pen on the table.[126]

A select committee is also not the right place to lounge around in a casual way, to pull faces or look generally disrespectful. I always say your body language should be as though you are at a job interview, where you try really hard to not send the wrong signals to the people you are trying to impress.

This is partly about controlling what you are doing with your hands. Use them to make your point, as good communicators do, but do not point, bang the table or wave people away. It will make you look arrogant and encourage an even tougher session.

One of the best (or worst!) examples of this was an appearance from the global pharmaceutical company Pfizer when it was seeking to acquire AstraZeneca. The senior executive representing the US company removed his jacket prior to sitting down, despite the fact he had not asked permission from the committee's chair. He even rolled up his sleeves and generally gave the impression of being supremely arrogant with his overly confident body language. Given that he was going into an already hostile environment (the MPs on the committee had begun the process highly sceptical about the intentions of the company), his terrible mannerisms and body language gave them further justification for giving him a hard time.

There are certain things beyond your control in a select committee, but how you present yourself is not one of them.

OPENING STATEMENT

I can't recall the training or planning for a select committee where I have not participated in a long, drawn-out discussion about whether an opening statement should be made by the witness. The usual format, when permitted, is for the witness to address the committee with a statement about the given issue. Sometimes the committee will give permission for this to happen, but it is always better to agree this well in advance of the hearing. Do not forget that the focus of the evidence session is on the committee putting questions to witnesses. The official guidance from Parliament is that 'committees generally prefer to get questioning immediately underway. Witnesses should, therefore, consider whether material to be covered in an opening statement can instead be provided to the committee in writing.'[127]

An opening statement should take no longer than a minute, because the worst thing that could happen is that the chair interrupts with a withering put-down, immediately putting you on the back foot, and setting a negative tone. Furthermore, you should try to learn the statement off by heart, even if you still have the written text in front of you as a handrail. Otherwise, it will appear that someone else has written it on your behalf, and this will inevitably hamper your efforts to present yourself as a witness willing to engage in a transparent way.

The upsides of doing an opening statement are:

- it allows you to say sorry early in the hearing, which is helpful if you know that the committee is going to demand an apology;
- it gives you control of the message you wish to convey;
- it may end up being the key broadcast clip, which is better than a moment in which you are being castigated; and
- it disciplines you, in advance, to better hone your key messages.

The downsides are:

- committees don't like them, even where they allow them;
- it makes you look too obviously trained and honed;
- it gets out all your key points within sixty seconds, and then you might have two hours to survive in which you have used up all your best lines; and
- the early apology sounds less sincere when read as part of an opening statement.

On balance, my advice is not to bother doing an opening statement.

ADDRESSING THE MEMBERS

When speaking to the committee members, the best method is to address the chair or co-chairs as 'chair' and other members as 'Mr' or 'Ms [surname]'. You should avoid being too casual – it is always safer to just stick to the formal system.

THE COMMITTEE ALWAYS WINS

During the course of questioning remember that there is little to be gained from taking too many risks or trying to gain an obvious victory over the committee. The MPs are both the opposing team and the referee, so it is difficult to beat them at their own game. That applies after the hearing too, when the committee can simply write up the report in the most aggressive, and personal, way possible to score an act of final revenge against you if you have bested them in the session itself.

I recall an instance when Margaret Hodge and her Public Accounts Committee were questioning the infamous payday lending industry. Having destroyed the big multinationals of Starbucks, Amazon and Google, surely a company willing to charge customers interest rates of 4,200 per cent would be easy? Unfortunately not. The representative of Wonga was very skilled at countering the committee's accusations one by one, with sharp facts delivered with merciless speed. The committee was left somewhat bemused as to how they had been bested in that particular encounter, and no doubt the witness felt very pleased with himself as he left Parliament. But, of course, the committee was able to have the last laugh by producing a report which tore apart that business's behaviour and attacked the veracity of his oral evidence. At that point, there is no right of reply.

HOW THE QUESTIONS ARE ASKED

Select committee questioning can be a shock for the unprepared, as it is rare to be grilled in such an obviously loaded way in almost any other walk of life. As I have highlighted previously, this is often not about getting to the truth or encouraging a thoughtful insight into any given issue. Rather, it is about scoring that winning goal in front of the cameras.

Your preparations will depend on the reason why you have been called. It is possible to be summoned as an expert witness, and this can be a perfectly pleasant experience. It could be that you represent a charity, are an economist, or are a victim of the issue. In those instances, you are likely to get a fairer hearing and often an easy time.

However, what you need to remember is that a select committee always has an enemy or target in mind. As an expert witness, you are helping the committee gather ammunition to shoot someone else down. The best thing to assume is that nothing is asked innocently.

One of the classic questions posed to allegedly wrongdoing CEOs is about their pay and benefits. A chair I interviewed explained why this is deployed: 'MPs are bothered by their salaries in comparison to the people they are questioning. We can't moan about it publicly but select committees offer an opportunity to vent this indirectly by being antagonistic about what witnesses earn.' For example, when Matt Brittin, a senior Google executive for the UK and Europe, went before a committee hearing on corporate tax structures in January 2016, he was ambushed in the first few minutes with questions about how much he is paid. Speaking to a former MP on the committee in question, Brittin was seen as an extremely adept witness and difficult to unpick. However, they scored one notable hit with the approach on wages.

As Google in the UK is not under any obligation to report his salary, Brittin had to endure an uncomfortable moment where it appeared that he did not know what he was paid. As you can imagine, the committee and the media had a field day with that answer (or lack of), even though it was broadly misunderstood.

Here is the transcript from that exchange:[128]

Chair: Do you hear the anger and frustration out there, because, with those huge [revenue] figures, you settled for a figure [tax payment to HMRC] of £130 million?

Matt Brittin: Absolutely, and I welcome the chance to come and talk to you about this. I understand the anger and—

Chair: Do you really understand the anger, Mr Brittin? What do you get paid, Mr Brittin?

Matt Brittin: If that is relevant, I will happily disclose that to the committee. What I understand is—

Chair: I am asking you what you get paid.

Matt Brittin: I will happily disclose that, if that's a relevant matter for the committee, in private.

Chair: I am asking you, so it is a relevant matter. Could you tell me what you get paid?

Matt Brittin: I don't have the figure, but I will happily provide it.

Chair: You don't know what you get paid, Mr Brittin?

Matt Brittin: Well, chair, let me—

Chair: Perhaps you could give us a ballpark figure for what you get paid. Forget the share options, then; what's your basic salary?

Matt Brittin: I don't have the figure, but I'll provide a figure privately if it's relevant to the committee to understand my salary. I would like to say—

Chair: Okay, you don't know what you get paid. My point is that out there, taxpayers – our constituents – are very angry.

Matt Brittin: I understand that.

Although the committee felt pleased it had landed a media hit on Brittin's apparent ignorance of his own salary, the rest of the hearing was smooth sailing for the Google executive.

As a former MP who took part in that session later told me, 'We skewered him on his pay issue, but it was admittedly a cheap shot which ultimately felt like a pyrrhic victory. He'll no doubt be pleased that we failed to land hits on his company's tax arrangements.'

This demonstrates how parliamentary committees often put style before substance when they ask questions. Everyone wants to be the star of the show, delivering the killer question which is seen to put the evasive witness to the sword.

However, there are a number of different styles that can be adopted. They can be grouped as:

- The Columbo question: Just as with the famous TV cop from the 1970s, some MPs seek to create a false sense of security in the witness by asking relatively helpful and seemingly constructive questions. Suddenly, they spring a 'just one more thing' surprise at the end which can catch the witness unawares.

- The relentless interrogator: This technique is to just persist with a line of questioning until the witness gives in or is beaten back by the chair.

- The surpriser: This person will seem relatively friendly until suddenly pulling out a letter from a constituent or an anonymous tip-off and put the witness directly on the spot to answer a very specific question, without any warning of its source or content.

The best-performing MPs on select committees don't tend to be those who just race off to attack and overreach with the ferocity of their questioning. The more dangerous ones lure the witness into a false sense of security with politeness and cool questioning, and then build an attack from the ground up.

Let's say an MP was trying to ascertain whether a CEO was paid an unacceptable amount of money. As an example, I shall use the former head of housebuilder Persimmon, who rose to fame when he was paid a bonus of £75 million and eventually refused to allow the media to even ask him about it (he departed the company soon after). It is only fair to note that he received £75 million, having originally been awarded over £100 million and he did eventually agree to give some of it to charity – but this was too little too late.

One way to challenge him would be to launch straight into an attack: 'Mr XXX, last year you were paid £75 million when millions of people struggle to make ends meet. Do you agree that it is a disgrace that you accepted the money?'

However, a more subtle and effective way is to build the argument more slowly but establish the facts along the way. For example, the question sequencing might be:

- 'Can you remind the committee how much you were paid in basic salary last year?' – This is to establish that the bonus is totally out of kilter compared with even his huge base salary.

- 'And how much was your bonus?' – The committee already knows but you ideally want the CEO to have to say it himself publicly.

- 'What were your performance measurements to achieve that bonus?' – The CEO will argue that the bonus amount was set by his remuneration committee, but let us give him the opportunity to try to justify it on a performance basis.

- 'What is the per cent pay gap between your total package and the lowest-paid back office employee in your business?' – Now we start to make him very embarrassed because the pay gap will be monstrous, perhaps £7 million versus £15,000–20,000.

- 'Did you consider saying no to the bonus, or at least to that actual amount?' – Now we start picking apart his lack of morals and ethics by accepting the money. Clearly, he could have.

- 'Will you now do the right thing and hand back some or all of your bonus?' – This is what the questioning builds up to, being an attempt to wear down the CEO until he blinks and makes a commitment to at least giving it further consideration.

The smart select committee quizzer does not launch straight into the key question, which the witness will be prepared to answer. In the example above, just simply asking if they deserved to be paid that monstrous bonus can be thwacked back with an easy answer about how it has been decided by an independent group of people on the board. It is much better, as I have demonstrated, to build the intensity, removing every safety net for the witness until they are left entirely exposed to public opinion.

CO-ORDINATION

It can often be confusing when there are multiple witnesses from the same organisation, who may struggle to co-ordinate as to who should take the question from the committee. Usually, the most senior witness (e.g. the CEO or minister) will have the question directed towards them in the first instance, with the others then permitted to come in to help with the answer. The key is to agree to a system in advance – if topic X comes up, the question should be answered by person Y. That saves a lot of time and prevents sloppy interplay between the witnesses, which can damage your credibility.

However, I would normally advise that the senior representative sometimes volunteers to the chair to take a question on which they have a strong hand. This shows leadership and is a good thing to do occasionally.

USE HANDRAILS

One of the techniques I use with every witness I train is to create 'handrails', which are there to help stabilise them in the event that the committee hearing begins to get out of control. Just as you use an actual handrail to stop yourself from falling, this can be an invaluable way to survive.

Here are some examples of handrails:

- A very clear and concise explanation of the company's purpose. For example, as company X is getting pummelled for supposedly unethical behaviour, you would remind the committee, 'This company has been in operation for more than 100 years and is active across all regions of the UK, employing 15,000 people, creating employment opportunities for young people and investing in local communities. We know we need to do better but

I believe we make a valuable contribution to society and I remain proud of the company I represent.'

- An outline of the actions you have already taken. You cannot win on the issue of the data breach, or the cancellation of thousands of flights, or any other major incident which has forced you to appear before the committee. However, you can certainly use a handrail which explains what you have subsequently done to fix the problem and to stop it happening again. For example, 'I entirely accept that we let down our customers on this occasion. We cannot change the past but let me tell you what we are doing to ensure it never happens again:

  1) We have initiated an independent review of what went wrong so we can learn the lessons.
  2) We will fully implement the results of those findings.
  3) We have created an early warning system which will make it less likely this incident could happen again.'

These handrails can be very important, given that the questions you are being asked can be wide-ranging and focus on almost any aspect of your business or organisation's activities. Having something to lean on is always helpful. This set of core principles and messages will help you if you find yourself struggling.

This technique is not about wasting the committee's time, it is about returning back to port if the ship is sailing into choppy waters and you think you might otherwise sink.

THE DON'TS

DON'T LIE

One thing I cannot stress enough is to never, under any circumstances, whatever the temptation, lie to a parliamentary committee. A lot of people outside of politics think that lying is what all its participants do every day. This is not actually true. Yes, they may be fairly accused of sometimes being disingenuous, but there is a subtle difference. A lie can get you out of the precise moment when you are on the ropes, but the consequences can be huge. Once you are positioned as a liar, you are seen to have lost the trust of the people with whom you interact and your reputation can take a long time to recover.

If you are caught out, the MPs on the committee (who spend their whole careers being labelled liars by a variety of opponents) will go for the jugular. This doesn't mean that you need to necessarily offer up every truthful detail of the issue on which you are being questioned. No one is forced to reveal information which has not been requested, and it is not your job to be so helpful that you deliver an easy, lazy victory for the committee. The task of extracting the killer information remains that of the committee. But if you are asked for a fact that is relevant to the inquiry, then ensure you do not produce a lie.

Deploying a lie to get you through a difficult set of questions from a group of MPs would give you only temporary relief from the onslaught, because once exposed, the lie will land you right back in front of the cameras for another session or, at best, a stinging letter or final committee report.

I had one such instance when I was working in-house, where we were training an unwilling chief executive. He was not remotely interested in politics, despite being in a very exposed industry which is reliant on keeping politicians onside. In our first meeting to discuss his appearance, we told him very clearly that he had to apportion some of the blame for the major error which triggered the inquiry to another company, as well as obviously apologising for his own performance. He refused to do the former and could not be budged, regardless of our urging and increasing exasperation. In short, he foolishly believed he was taking the moral high ground and would emerge with some credit for doing so.

This was bad enough, as inevitably the other company executive was extremely smart and pinned all the blame on his counterpart and the company managed to escape the sharpest criticism. But worse than that, our CEO's attempts to be 'honourable' led him to lie, which subsequently came to light and would haunt him for months to come. Once the committee realised they had been misled, the chief executive was hauled back in for a humiliating second session all by himself. Unsurprisingly, it was less an opportunity to find out further information and more about teaching him a lesson. Not only was that a gruelling experience in itself, but the committee's final report on the issue specifically name-checked the individual and all but called him out as a liar. Fortunately for him, social media was not a major force at that time. If it had been, there would have been live tweets chronicling his abject failure and it would inevitably have been noticed to a much greater extent by other politicians and the media. This type of scrutiny could have left an indelible stain on his character. You may not be so lucky.

Even refusing to answer questions from a committee can find you in contempt of Parliament, which can have significant reputational consequences. When Oliver Robbins, then second Permanent Secretary of the Home Office (and more recently the Prime Minister's key Brexit negotiator), was thrown out of an evidence session before the Home Affairs Committee in 2016, the chair suggested that the committee might hold him in contempt for failing to answer its questions about the budget of the UK Border Force. Subsequently, having not provided the committee with further details in response to their questions by a 6 p.m. deadline, Robbins was asked to appear before the committee again a few days later.

According to the Institute for Government, the government's view (notably one never endorsed by Parliament) is that civil servants appearing before committees do so as representatives of ministers and under their instruction. Consequently, it is for ministers to decide which civil servant should represent them or whether they would prefer to appear themselves, which could have been a possibility in this instance.[129]

The fact that the Home Affairs Committee went as far as ordering a senior civil servant to leave the evidence session demonstrates that its longstanding frustrations about its ability to extract information from government and hold civil servants to account continue to be unresolved.

DON'T BE PARTISAN

Given the relative political balance of all select committees, make sure not to make overtly partisan points about the government, opposition or other smaller parties, even if specifically encouraged by a committee member. Most MPs are surprisingly respectful to one another in these instances, but just occasionally a newbie to the committee might see an opportunity to impress their party's bosses. Your job is to stick to a cool assessment of the facts, especially where it relates to party policy. You might curry favour with one or two MPs by supporting them, but then alienate many others. In short, leave your own politics outside the committee room door. If you can demonstrate that a policy challenge is the result of successive governments, then all the better.

AVOID EMPTY PROMISES

Do not, under any circumstances, be tempted to give commitments that you have no intention of living up to outside the room. There may be a temptation to do so in order to extricate yourself from that immediate moment of pressure, but it will cause a major problem further down the line.

The best (and worst) example is Irene Rosenfeld, the former Kraft CEO, who prompted a furore after she announced in 2011 that the company would close a plant in Somerdale, near Bristol, with the loss of nearly 500 jobs. The previous owners, Cadbury, had already announced plans to close the plant and shift production to Poland, but during the takeover battle, Kraft promised it would keep the factory open. This was a major attraction for those who feared a foreign takeover of a much-loved British institution. To have seemingly blatantly lied to gain an edge in the takeover battle (afterwards Kraft claimed that the move to Poland was too advanced to reverse) may have helped in the very short term, but the impact on Kraft's reputation still resonates today. Even more than the damage for this specific company, the factory closure continues to be a totemic example of corporate wrongdoing during foreign takeovers, which played a major part in changes to the UK's competition regime, both formally and informally.

MPs also complained that Rosenfeld had snubbed them by not attending the Business, Energy and Industrial Strategy Committee hearing in person. She instead sent Kraft's executive vice-president, Marc Firestone, who looked visibly stunned by the hammering he received from the committee. He said he was 'terribly sorry' that hopes had been raised and then dashed over Somerdale, and that Rosenfeld had been unable to attend due to a board meeting but 'had the deepest respect' for the UK Parliament. He said the original pledge had been made in 'good faith'.[130]

You may think you have dodged a bullet by saying what is necessary to get out of the room in one piece, but it is inevitable that you will be held to account eventually if you have made a pledge you have no intention of delivering on.

Empty promises are often made due to a loss of composure, which you must try to maintain regardless of what is thrown at you during the session. Do not lose your temper with members at any point, even if they are trying to provoke you, which they usually will try to do. Remember that MPs often have half an eye on their own profile, so some grandstanding should be expected – the key is to ignore it and keep coolly focused on responding in the right way.

DON'T REPEAT

If you are appearing alongside a number of other witnesses on the same panel, especially if you are from the same organisation, try not to repeat what another person has just said. If you agree with a point which has just been made, then feel free to say so and move on rather than ramble in the hope of wasting time. It may seem as though it could provide some breathing space, but committee chairs know all the tricks and will make an intervention to move the discussion on, often criticising you in the process.

DO NOT PATRONISE

From the interviews I conducted with senior select committee chairs, both past and present, it seems that they all get extremely irritated by a witness's attempts to curry favour with compliments. The most obvious way of doing this is to say, 'That's a great question,' which just comes across as the worst kind of toadying behaviour. The chairs know that any difficult question will not be considered 'great' by a witness, and they react badly to flattery.

Another issue is one of which male witnesses in particular need to be wary. In recent years, there has been a far greater awareness of interactions between men and women in public life. If there is any suspicion that a male witness is talking down to a female MP, or, for example, treating her as though she is unable to grasp the complexity of the business or the implications of an issue, he will be ruthlessly punished.

The common term nowadays is 'mansplaining', which entered the language around 2010. In fact, it was named one of the words of the year by the *New York Times*[131] (am I now mansplaining this to you?). One of the female committee chairs I interviewed specifically used this term and said it has happened to her in committee sessions on a number of occasions. She felt it was a combination of 'cluelessness and overconfidence' that leads some male business leaders to patronise a female audience. Either way, you will be on a hiding to nothing. This does not mean you should not seek to communicate as simply and clearly as possible, but always be mindful of the people you are speaking to in a committee hearing and pitch your explanations to the right level. Doing an appropriate amount of homework about the individual members prior to entering the room can only help your preparations.

AVOID JARGON AND CLICHÉS

During your preparations, you should spend time practising and honing your communication skills. The ability to bring to life a complex issue in a simple way is a really important skill, by using clear and concise language and avoiding technical or overly fancy phrasing. Whenever I am training witnesses, I find myself having to repeatedly remind them that the jargon which is second nature in their own industry will be hated by a parliamentary committee. I know this seems a bit rich given that politicians are famous for their ability to dodge a question, but jargon does seem to especially irritate them. I think it is partly because not understanding the acronyms can make the committee feel stupid for not knowing what they mean.

The avoidance of jargon is not just for the committee's benefit. MPs tend to be generalists, rather than specialists, but it is also a complete turn-off for members of the public who may be watching. It is therefore important to stick to simple and clear language.

There is also a trend of companies with a US link using certain business phrases which can irritate a cynical British committee. These business clichés do become a force of habit after a while, but it is important to safeguard against their use in front of a UK audience. Let me give you some of my personal 'favourites', all of which I have heard deployed by witnesses in Parliament:

- Burning platform – something which is considered urgent and important.
- Boil the ocean – undertaking an impossible task or one which is too difficult to make it worthwhile.
- Low-hanging fruit – the easiest and most achievable set of tasks.
- Reaching out – to communicate with a person or group of people.
- Going forwards – something to take place in the future.

I know – they look even more ridiculous when written down. Just do not use them in a select committee, ever. Full stop.

Additionally, sometimes companies refer to their employees with a distinctive name invented for internal audiences. For example, Starbucks call their staff 'partners' ('Being a Starbucks Partner means you are more than just an employee – you are a member of our inclusive partner community');[132] Nando's call theirs 'Nandocas' ('the name we give to every member of our family').[133] This is, of course, perfectly acceptable within the internal culture of those companies, but for the purposes of appearing before a committee, it is better to stick with formal titles.

AFTER THE SESSION

WRITING TO THE COMMITTEE

There is an established convention that if you are struggling for information or an answer, you can offer to write to the committee with the requested information following the session. If you do not have the information to answer a question immediately to hand, it is perfectly reasonable for you to get it right later rather than mislead the committee unintentionally.

This method is not appropriate if the question is about your opinion or your own recollection of events. It will be along the lines of a question such as, 'What was the average bonus for board-level executives in 2017?', which may require some research after the hearing is over. It is often not a stat or item of data you want to risk guessing. However, this opportunity to write to the committee can only be used sparingly, otherwise you may seem clueless, or as though you do know the answer but are buying yourself time to run down the clock.

You will need to send any further information which you have agreed to provide to the committee staff as soon as possible. The committee's officials will usually follow up with you afterwards via email, reminding you of the additional information which you promised to provide. This information is ordinarily treated as written evidence and published alongside other such evidence received by the committee.

However, it is a good idea to make the first contact, in the spirit of being transparent and helpful, with an email or letter which might look like this:

Dear [name of chair],

Thank you for inviting me to provide evidence to your committee earlier this week. As part of your questioning, you asked me for further information on XXX and YYY.

I am delighted to attach the data you requested, and if there are any further questions arising from it, do please let me know.

Yours sincerely,

[Name of witness]

An expanded version of the letter or email (using the example of a company being quizzed on its general corporate behaviour in the UK) might look like this:

Dear [name of chair],

Thank you for having invited me to give evidence to your committee. I hope I was able to provide the information which members required as you take forward your inquiry.

*During the session, there were three occasions where I
was not in a position to answer with complete accuracy
and I promised to write to the committee to provide that
information.*

*On the question of our total tax receipts for the financial
year 2012/13, I can confirm we paid £14 million in corporation tax.*

*In regards to the question about the date on which I first
received an email highlighting the event unfolding, I can
confirm that it was from our director of HR on 13 June 2013.*

*You asked how many redundancies we announced in
July 2013. I can confirm that 238 people accepted the offer
of redundancy, with the majority choosing to take this on a
voluntary basis.*

*If there are any further questions you may have, please
do not hesitate to contact me on XXX.*

Yours sincerely,

[Name of witness]

There have been occasions when the committee has not followed up, but this is rare, and is usually only because the
chair decides they did not really care to find out the answer.

FOLLOW-UP

A couple of days afterwards, as you recover from the experience, you will be sent an uncorrected transcript by the clerk,
which you should check and return. However, this is not an

opportunity for you to rewrite history. This is purely to check for factual errors in the transcript. For example, if it states that 'company X divested itself of its assets in India in 2009 for £4.5 billion' when the reality is 'company X divested itself of its assets in India in 2011 for £2.5 billion' then a correction can be approved, or you should suggest a footnote be appended.

The committee will publish its report at a later date (often weeks or months later). You can ask to see an embargoed copy a day before publication, which may be granted and sent to the person who originally either submitted the written evidence on behalf of the company or was the key witness in the hearing.

If you were the witness giving evidence, having someone externally providing some quick feedback after the event is a good idea. You will be anxious to know how it seemed to people outside of the room. Hopefully, they will dwell as much as possible on the positives. After all, the session has been completed and there is little point picking holes in everything you may have got wrong. That is something you will be likely to realise anyway.

However, there may be issues that require a follow-up with the committee to smooth over a problem that arose, and this can be managed through the committee's officials.

GOVERNMENT RESPONSE

The government has a formal duty to respond to select committee reports where they ask questions of specific departments or policies. This, however, excludes instances where a company has done wrong, and which cannot be the responsibility of the government – for example, a bank losing its customers' data, or the botched opening of a new airport terminal. As explored in Part 2, the government is usually given up to sixty days from the date a final report is published to respond, to which the committee can later reply if it wishes to further push its key points.

The government replies are usually fairly anodyne – this is certainly not seen as a forum for major policy announcements or concessions. The government will also have a fairly good idea way in advance as to what a committee is going to conclude, so officials and political advisors can begin planning the response over an extended time.

I have always felt that committees miss a trick by not being sharper with government responses to the inquiries. Again, putting on my cynical hat (is it ever off?), I feel that many committees have lost interest in the inquiry by the time the government has got round to responding. The timetable for committees is always tight and therefore the chairs will have considered the job is already done, and have moved on to the next topic of inquiry.

There is a formal process of responding, and officials in the relevant department(s) will be working away to source data for the answers and policy steer from the ministers and advisors. However, the committees need to keep the pressure on if they wish to spur the government into action. Although in Part 1 we ascertained that around a third of departmental select committee recommendations are adopted by government, so much more could be achieved by doing even more to hold departments to account weeks and months after the end of an inquiry.

At the end of your select committee process, you will feel exhausted. You will certainly feel relieved that it is over and you can return to your normal daily routine. Hopefully few people noticed that you gave evidence, and you said nothing which will subsequently damage your career and reputation. When a session goes without a hitch, I find that the witnesses I help train start to feel a real pride that they have experienced and survived a select committee. In the words of one witness I trained in 2018:

> The first twenty minutes of the session felt really uncomfortable but the remaining forty minutes flew by. I left the committee room with no real idea whether it had gone well. Gradually, over a celebratory pint that afternoon, I relaxed and felt that I had achieved something. They should make T-shirts for select committee survivors!

ENDNOTES

1   Professor Meg Russell and Meghan Benton, 'Selective Influence: The Policy Impact of House of Commons Select Committees', The Constitution Unit, UCL, June 2011, https://www.ucl.ac.uk/constitution-unit/sites/constitution-unit/files/153.pdf

2   Philip Aylett, 'Thirty Years of Reform: House of Commons Select Committees, 1960–1990', https://qmro.qmul.ac.uk/xmlui/bitstream/handle/123456789/18377/Aylett_P_PhD_final_230516.pdf?sequence=1

3   Ibid.

4   https://www.parliament.uk/business/committees/committees-a-z/commons-select/public-accounts-committee/role/

5   Hansard, HC Deb, 30 November 1961, vol. 650, col. 641.

6   Philip Aylett, 'Thirty Years of Reform: House of Commons Select Committees, 1960–1990', https://qmro.qmul.ac.uk/xmlui/bitstream/handle/123456789/18377/Aylett_P_PhD_final_230516.pdf?sequence=1

7   Ibid.

8   Ibid.

9   Ibid.

10 'Rebuilding the House', Reform of the House of Commons Select Committee, 24 November 2009, https://publications.parliament.uk/pa/cm200809/cmselect/cmrefhoc/1117/111702.htm

11 https://www.instituteforgovernment.org.uk/publication/parliamentary-monitor-2018/select-committees

12 https://www.parliament.uk/about/how/committees/joint/

13 https://www.instituteforgovernment.org.uk/publication/parliamentary-monitor-2018/select-committees

14 Nick Reeve, 'Politicians to probe UK universities pension scheme', IPE, 23 August 2017.

15 'Rachel Reeves elected as Chair', 12 July 2017, https://www.parliament.uk/business/committees/committees-a-z/commons-select/business-energy-industrial-strategy/news-parliament-2017/chair-elected-17-19/

16 Johnny Mercer, 'Select committee chairs are too important to "play politics" with', *The Times*, 12 July 2017.
17 Dr Hannah White, 'Selecting the select committees – what happens next?', Institute for Government, 19 May 2015.
18 https://www.instituteforgovernment.org.uk/blog/selecting-select-committees-%E2%80%93-what-happens-next
19 https://www.instituteforgovernment.org.uk/publication/parliamentary-monitor-2018/select-committees
20 Richard Kelly, 'Select committees: election of chairs and members', Briefing Paper 7176, 14 July 2017.
21 'Guide for Select Committee Members', House of Commons, June 2017, https://www.parliament.uk/documents/commons-committees/guide-select-ctte-members.pdf
22 Ibid.
23 https://www.instituteforgovernment.org.uk/publication/parliamentary-monitor-2018/select-committees
24 Ibid.
25 Mari Takayanagi, 'Parliament and Women c1900– 1945', King's College London, https://kclpure.kcl.ac.uk/portal/files/30807371/2012_Takayanagi_Mari_1069335_ethesis.pdf
26 Oonagh Gay, '1957 – A glass ceiling shattered!', UK Vote 100, 7 November 2017.
27 https://www.instituteforgovernment.org.uk/publication/parliamentary-monitor-2018/select-committees
28 John Johnston, 'Fresh Brexit committee split over "Norway-style" trade proposal' PoliticsHome, 4 April 2018.
29 Juliette Jowit, 'Rupert Murdoch "not fit" verdict was proposed six weeks before MPs' vote', *The Guardian*, 2 May 2012.
30 'The Accountability of Civil Servants', Constitution Committee – Sixth Report, Chapter Four: Accountability of Civil Servants to Parliament, 7 November 2012.
31 'Giving Evidence to Select Committees: Guidance for Civil Servants', Cabinet Office, October 2014.
32 Ibid.
33 Andy Bloxham, 'Parliamentary privilege: a guide', *Daily Telegraph*, 10 November 2010.
34 'Select Committees are Becoming the Ugly Face of Parliament: It's Time to Rein Them In', The Royal Society of Arts, 4 February 2013.
35 https://www.parliament.uk/business/committees/committees-archive/international-development/guide-for-witnesses/.
36 http://news.bbc.co.uk/1/hi/uk_politics/3466005.stm
37 https://www.parliament.uk/business/parliament-tv/parliament-live-help/
38 Andrew Sparrow, 'Cabinet to meet outside London', *The Guardian*, 4 August 2008.
39 Annabelle Dickson, 'Taxpayer foots £84,000 for "fake news" US trip bill', Politico, 13 March 2018.
40 'Committee visit to New York and Washington DC Freedom of Information

request', 13 March 2018, https://www.parliament.uk/business/committees/committees-a-z/commons-select/digital-culture-media-and-sport-committee/news/us-visit-foi/

41 Annabelle Dickson, 'Taxpayer foots £84,000 for "fake news" US trip bill', Politico, 13 March 2018.

42 'Gwyneth Dunwoody', Obituaries, *The Guardian*, 18 April 2008.

43 https://publications.parliament.uk/pa/cm200708/cmselect/cmtran/53/7101002.htm

44 Edward Pearce, 'Gwyneth Dunwoody', *The Guardian*, 19 April 2008.

45 Donald Macintyre, 'Andrew Tyrie: The most powerful backbencher in the House of Commons', *The Independent*, 2 April 2013.

46 George Parker, 'Tyrie aims to bring "Sun King" down to earth', *Financial Times*, 26 January 2012.

47 John Crace, 'David Cameron sees red as the liaison committee bares its teeth', *The Guardian*, 12 January 2016.

48 Rowena Mason, 'Brief, brutal and very public: there's more to Margaret Hodge's grillings than dramatics', *The Guardian*, 13 March 2015.

49 'A Point of View: Do parliament's select committees wield too much power?', BBC News, 22 March 2015.

50 Peter Riddell, 'The Hodge question: to whom are civil servants accountable?', Institute for Government, 19 March 2012.

51 Helia Ebrahimi and Harry Watson, 'Margaret Hodge's family company pays just 0.01pc tax on £2.1bn of business generated in the UK', *Daily Telegraph*, 9 November 2012.

52 Rajeev Syal, 'Margaret Hodge stands aside as head of spending watchdog', *The Guardian*, 20 May 2015.

53 Patrick Mercer, 'Eleventh Report of Session 2013–2014', HC 1225, House of Commons Committee on Standards, 1 May 2014.

54 Nick Dorman and Dan Warburton, 'Keith Vaz branded a "liar" by male escorts as they reveal shamed MP offered to fly them around world', *Sunday Mirror*, 10 September 2016.

55 Tom Bergin, 'Special Report: How Starbucks avoids UK taxes', Reuters, 15 October 2012.

56 Jamie Grierson, 'Ground down: Starbucks pledges to pay £20 million tax over next two years', *The Independent*, 6 December 2012.

57 Coral Garnick, 'Former Starbucks exec Troy Alstead has a new gig', *Puget Sound Business Journal*, 29 March 2017.

58 http://www.bbc.co.uk/news/av/business-20301381/mps-condemn-amazon-executive-over-tax-payments

59 Public Accounts Committee – Minutes of Evidence, HC 716, 12 November 2012, https://publications.parliament.uk/pa/cm201213/cmselect/cmpubacc/716/121112.htm

60 Gerry Holt, 'G4S staff hit out over Olympics security "shambles"', BBC News, 18 July 2012.

61 Szu Ping Chan, 'Timeline: how G4S's bungled Olympics security contract unfolded', *Daily Telegraph*, 21 May 2013.

62   'G4S Boss Nick Buckles To Quit After Olympic Games Security Fiasco', Huff-Post, 21 May 2015.
63   Uncorrected Transcript of Oral Evidence, HC 531, 17 July 2012, https://publications.parliament.uk/pa/cm201213/cmselect/cmhaff/uc531-i/uc53101.htm
64   Rupert Neate, 'G4S boss stays but two lieutenants go after Olympics shambles', The Guardian, 28 September 2012.
65   Nick Davies, 'Police "ignored News of the World phone hacking evidence"', The Guardian, 4 April 2010.
66   'Phone-hacking: Hayman overreacts to payments questioning', Daily Telegraph, 12 July 2011.
67   Unauthorised tapping into or hacking of mobile communications, Uncorrected Typescript of Oral Evidence, HC 907-v, 12 July 2011, https://publications.parliament.uk/pa/cm201012/cmselect/cmhaff/uc907-v/uc90701.htm
68   Matthew Norman, 'The good, the bad and the downright thick', Daily Telegraph, 15 July 2011.
69   Simon Hoggart, 'Andy Hayman stars at phone-hacking committee session', The Guardian, 12 July 2011.
70   'Unauthorised tapping into or hacking of mobile communications', HC 907, House of Commons Home Affairs Committee, 20 July 2011, https://www.parliament.uk/documents/commons-committees/home-affairs/unauthorised-tapping-or-hacking-mobile-communications-report.pdf
71   'FA questioned on ability to conduct internal investigations', Digital, Culture, Media and Sport Committee, 22 September 2017, https://www.parliament.uk/business/committees/committees-a-z/commons-select/digital-culture-media-and-sport-committee/news/governance-fa-evidence-17-19/
72   Oral evidence: Sport Governance, HC 320, Digital, Culture, Media and Sport Committee, 18 October 2017, http://data.parliament.uk/writtenevidence/committeeevidence.svc/evidencedocument/digital-culture-media-and-sport-committee/sport-governance/oral/71851.html
73   'BHS files for administration', BBC News, 25 April 2016.
74   Chris Johnston, 'Sir Philip Green calls for Frank Field to resign', The Guardian, 11 June 2016.
75   Oral evidence: The Pension Protection Fund and Pensions Regulator, HC 55, Work and Pensions Committee and Business, Innovation and Skills Committee, 15 June 2016, http://data.parliament.uk/writtenevidence/committeeevidence.svc/evidencedocument/work-and-pensions-committee/pension-protection-fund-and-the-pensions-regulator/oral/34431.html
76   Oral evidence: Fake News, HC 363, Digital, Culture, Media and Sport Committee, 12 Jun 2018, http://data.parliament.uk/writtenevidence/committeeevidence.svc/evidencedocument/digital-culture-media-and-sport-committee/disinformation-and-fake-news/oral/85344.html
77   Damian Collins, 'Arron Banks's bullyboy tactics will not stop me pursuing the truth', The Guardian, 31 October 2018.
78   'A History of Notable Senate Investigations', United States Senate, https://www.senate.gov/artandhistory/history/common/briefing/Investigations.htm
79   'Parliamentary committees of inquiry in national systems: a comparative

survey of EU Member States', Citizens' Rights and Constitutional Affairs Policy Department, EU Parliament, http://www.europarl.europa.eu/RegData/etudes/note/join/2011/462427/IPOL-AFCO_NT(2011)462427_EN.pdf

80 Michael D. Bopp and Noam Noked (co-editor), 'Investigative Authorities of House and Senate Committees', Harvard Law School Forum on Corporate Governance and Financial Regulation, 14 August 2011.

81 https://www.aph.gov.au/About_Parliament/House_of_Representatives/Powers_practice_and_procedure/00_-_Infosheets/Infosheet_4_-_Committees

82 'Object Lessons: Parliamentary Committees Abroad, Their Functions and Powers', Memorandum from Democratic Audit, Human Rights Centre, University of Essex, Appendix 24, Modernisation of the House of Commons Committee Minutes of Evidence, 12 February 2002, https://publications.parliament.uk/pa/cm200102/cmselect/cmmodern/224/224ap25.htm

83 https://www.parliament.nz/en/document/00HOOOCPubResAboutFact-SheetsSelect1#_Toc266188600

84 Steve Barclay, 'Are Parliament's select committees working? – I say no', The Spectator, 5 November 2013.

85 https://www.instituteforgovernment.org.uk/publication/parliamentary-monitor-2018/select-committees

86 'BBC pay-offs: MPs condemn "cronyism"', BBC News, 16 December 2013.

87 Written evidence from the Clerk of the House of Commons, SEL0001, February 2017, http://data.parliament.uk/writtenevidence/committeeevidence.svc/evidencedocument/committee-of-privileges/select-committee-powers/written/48435.html

88 https://www.parliament.uk/business/committees/committees-a-z/commons-select/privileges/inquiries/parliament-2015/select-committee-powers-16-17/

89 'The powers of select committees and contempt examined', Committee of Privileges, 7 March 2017, https://www.parliament.uk/business/committees/committees-a-z/commons-select/privileges/news/select-committee-powers-inquiry-launch-16-17/

90 Universal Credit: early progress, House of Commons Committee of Public Accounts,7 November 2013, https://publications.parliament.uk/pa/cm201314/cmselect/cmpubacc/619/619.pdf

91 https://www.instituteforgovernment.org.uk/publication/parliamentary-monitor-2018/select-committees

92 Written evidence from the Clerk of the House of Commons (SEL0001), February 2017, http://data.parliament.uk/writtenevidence/committeeevidence.svc/evidencedocument/committee-of-privileges/select-committee-powers/written/48435.html

93 Ibid.

94 Ibid.

95 https://www.instituteforgovernment.org.uk/blog/contempt-witnesses-select-committees

96 https://www.instituteforgovernment.org.uk/publication/parliamentary-monitor-2018/summary

97 'Regional Accountability', House of Commons Select Committee on Modernisation

of the House of Commons, 10 July 2008, https://publications.parliament.uk/pa/cm200708/cmselect/cmmodern/282/282.pdf

98 Ibid.

99 'EU referendum: The result in maps and charts', BBC News, 24 June 2016.

100 Written evidence submitted by Dr Marc Geddes (SCP 08), December 2018, http://data.parliament.uk/writtenevidence/committeeevidence.svc/evidencedocument/procedure-committee/establishing-select-committees-in-a-new-parliament/written/93728.html

101 Steve Barclay, 'Are Parliament's select committees working? – I say no', *The Spectator*, 5 November 2013.

102 https://www.instituteforgovernment.org.uk/publication/parliamentary-monitor-2018/select-committees

103 'Rebuilding the House – Conclusions and Recommendations', 24 November 2009, https://publications.parliament.uk/pa/cm200809/cmselect/cmrefhoc/1117/111711.htm

104 https://www.instituteforgovernment.org.uk/publication/parliamentary-monitor-2018/select-committees

105 'Ministerial Code', Cabinet Office, January 2018, https://assets.publishing.service.gov.uk/government/uploads/system/uploads/attachment_data/file/672633/2018-01-08_MINISTERIAL_CODE_JANUARY_2018__FINAL___3_.pdf

106 Andy Hiller, 'MPs reject Baroness Stowell as next Charity Commission chair', Third Sector, 21 February 2018.

107 Hansard, HC Deb, 21 November 1989, vol. 162, cc7-103.

108 Marina Hyde, 'Why bring Russell Brand to testify to a select committee instead of an expert witness?', *The Guardian*, 26 April 2012.

109 Matthew Treadwell, 'Gary Neville says the FA would regret selling Wembley Stadium', Sky News, 18 July 2018.

110 'Russell Brand questioned for drugs policy inquiry', Home Affairs Select Committee, 24 April 2012, http://www.parliament.uk/business/committees/committees-a-z/commons-select/home-affairs-committee/news/120424-drugs-oral-ev/

111 'Lights, camera, action! Celebs at select committees', Total Politics, 14 September 2012.

112 Committee questions celebrities, Ofcom and Press Complaints Commission, Joint Committee on Privacy and Injunctions, 5 December 2011, https://www.parliament.uk/business/committees/committees-a-z/former-committees/joint-select/privacy-and-superinjunctions/news/evidence-session-5-december/

113 Communities and Local Government Committee question Mary Portas, 2 September 2013, https://www.parliament.uk/business/committees/committees-a-z/commons-select/communities-and-local-government-committee/news/ask-portas1/

114 Alexandra Topping, 'BBC stars faced huge tax bills after "having to set up companies"', *The Guardian*, 20 March 2018.

115 https://www.instituteforgovernment.org.uk/publication/parliamentary-monitor-2018/select-committees

116 Ibid.

117 'Establishing select committees in a new Parliament inquiry', https://www.parliament.uk/business/committees/committees-a-z/commons-select/procedure-committee/inquiries/parliament-2017/establishing-select-committess-17-19/

118 https://www.instituteforgovernment.org.uk/publication/parliamentary-monitor-2018/select-committees

119 'Establishing select committees in a new Parliament inquiry', https://www.parliament.uk/business/committees/committees-a-z/commons-select/procedure-committee/inquiries/parliament-2017/establishing-select-committess-17-19/

120 Written evidence submitted by Neil Parish MP, Chairman of the Environment, Food and Rural Affairs Committee, SCP 05, 25 June 2018, http://data.parliament.uk/writtenevidence/committeeevidence.svc/evidencedocument/procedure-committee/establishing-select-committees-in-a-new-parliament/written/86261.html

121 'Written evidence submitted by Dr Marc Geddes, SCP 08, December 2018, http://data.parliament.uk/writtenevidence/committeeevidence.svc/evidencedocument/procedure-committee/establishing-select-committees-in-a-new-parliament/written/93728.html

122 'Karen Bradley faces calls to resign over Troubles comments', BBC News, 6 March 2019.

123 Harry Cole, 'Cabinet newbie Jeremy Wright savaged after boasting he doesn't spend a penny on newspapers', *The Sun*, 6 November 2018.

124 'Guide for witnesses giving written or oral evidence to a House of Commons select committee', House of Commons, updated February 2016, https://www.parliament.uk/documents/commons-committees/witnessguide.pdf

125 'Who, what, why: What is the parliamentary dress code?', BBC News, 30 October 2014.

126 Philip Houston, Michael Floyd and Susan Carnicero, *Spy the Lie* (New York: St Martin's Press, 2012).

127 'Guide for witnesses giving written or oral evidence to a House of Commons select committee', House of Commons, updated February 2016, https://www.parliament.uk/documents/commons-committees/witnessguide.pdf.

128 Oral evidence: Corporate tax deals, HC 788, Public Accounts Committee, 11 February 2016, http://data.parliament.uk/writtenevidence/committeeevidence.svc/evidencedocument/public-accounts-committee/corporate-tax-deals/oral/28885.html

129 Dr Hannah White, 'In contempt? Witnesses before select committees', Institute for Government, 18 April 2016.

130 House of Commons Oral Evidence taken before the Business Innovation and Skills Committee, Uncorrected Transcript of Oral Evidence, HC 871-i, 15 March 2011, https://publications.parliament.uk/pa/cm201011/cmselect/cmbis/uc871-i/uc87101.htm

131 Sam Sefton and Grant Bennett, 'The Words of the Year', *New York Times*, 18 December 2010.

132 https://www.starbucks.co.uk/responsibility/socialimpact/beingapartner

133 http://careers.nandos.co.uk/roles/nandocas/

ABOUT THE AUTHOR

Scott Colvin is a partner and director of public affairs at global communications firm Finsbury and has prepared over 100 senior executives for some of the highest-profile select committee hearings of the past twenty years. He is the author of *How to Use Politicians to Get What You Want*, which won the prestigious Atticus award in 2012.